PEARSON

ALWAYS LEARNING

Townsend • Keator

Skills for Success

with Computer Concepts, Microsoft® Internet Explorer® 9, and Windows® 7

Custom Edition for Miami Dade College – Kendall Campus, CGS 1060

Taken from:
Skills for Success with Computer Concepts: Getting Started
by Kris Townsend and Vonda Keator

Skills for Success with Microsoft® Internet Explorer® 9: Getting Started
by Kris Townsend

Skills for Success with Windows® 7: Getting Started
by Kris Townsend

Cover Art: Courtesy of Photodisc/Getty Images.

Taken from:
Skills for Success with Computer Concepts: Getting Started
by Kris Townsend and Vonda Keator
Copyright 2012 by Pearson Education, Inc.
Published by Prentice Hall
Upper Saddle River, New Jersey 07458

Skills for Success with Microsoft® Internet Explorer® 9: Getting Started
by Kris Townsend
Copyright 2012 by Pearson Education, Inc.
Published by Prentice Hall

Skills for Success with Windows® 7: Getting Started
by Kris Townsend
Copyright 2011 by Pearson Education, Inc.
Published by Prentice Hall

Pearson Learning Solutions, 501 Boylston Street, Suite 900, Boston, MA 02116
A Pearson Education Company
www.pearsoned.com

Printed in the United States of America

10 V064 17 16 15 14 13

000200010271657508

TS

ISBN 10: 1-256-76720-4
ISBN 13: 978-1-256-76720-6

Table of Contents

Skills for Success with Windows® 7: Getting Started
by Kris Townsend

More Skills

CHAPTER 1

Basic Computer Concepts

▶ This chapter looks at different types of computers and their functions. It discusses computer hardware and software and the benefits of networking.

▶ In addition, this chapter discusses the importance of safe computing practices and the ways that you can protect your computer from various threats.

OBJECTIVES

At the end of this chapter you will be able to:

Objective 1	Identify the Four Basic Computing Functions
Objective 2	Identify the Different Types of Computers
Objective 3	Describe Hardware Devices and Their Uses
Objective 4	Identify Types of Software and Their Uses
Objective 5	Describe Networks and Define Network Terms
Objective 6	Identify Safe Computing Practices

In this chapter, you will learn about various types of computers. You will also be able to identify the components that make up a computer such as its hardware and software, and you will learn what a network is and how a computer can be used.

Introduction

▶ Computers are an integral part of our lives. They are found in homes, offices, stores, hospitals, libraries, and many other places. Computers are part of cars and phones, and they enable you to access bank accounts from home, shop online, and quickly communicate with people around the world by means of email and the Internet. It is difficult to find a business or occupation that doesn't rely on computers. Whether it's a truck driver who keeps an electronic travel log or a high-powered stockbroker who needs up-to-the-second market information, computers can make these tasks faster, easier, more efficient, and more accurate.

▶ Computers are all around us, which makes it important to learn basic computing skills and gain the knowledge to be a responsible computer user.

► Four basic computer functions—input, process, output, and store data—work together in order to process and present information in a meaningful manner.

What are the benefits of becoming computer competent? One advantage of being computer competent is that it makes employees more attractive to potential employers. Because computers have changed the way we work, as listed in **Figure 1**, many employers expect employees to have basic computer skills when they are hired.

In addition, if you are knowledgeable about computers and their uses, it makes you a better consumer. You will feel more comfortable when it comes to purchasing the right computer hardware and software for your needs, adding a peripheral for a specific use, or detecting basic problems when a system does not work properly. If you have a basic understanding of today's technology, you can also better understand and use *new* technologies.

What are the basic functions of a computer? A *computer* is a programmable electronic device that can input, process, output, and store data. The term *programmable* means that a device can be instructed to perform a task or a function when fed with a program or software.

A computer takes data and converts it into information. *Data* represents text, numbers, graphics, sounds, and videos entered into the computer's memory during input operations. *Information* is data that has been processed so that it can be presented in an organized and

■ **Continue to the next page to complete the objective.** ▶

- The traditional memo has given way to email messages.

- Business reports can now be shared on a network, enabling a group of individuals to collaborate by adding their own notes and comments before the report is finalized.

- Presentation graphic software is widely used to share information with an audience in a conference room or via the company's intranet.

- Spreadsheet software is a key tool in presenting financial information and developing sound business plans.

Figure 1 How computers have changed the way we work.

Figure 2 Being computer competent makes you more attractive to potential employers and a better consumer.

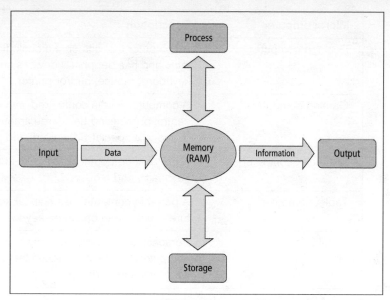

Figure 3 These are the four computer functions within the information processing cycle. *Memory* is not considered a function, but it is the center of flow of data and information within this cycle.

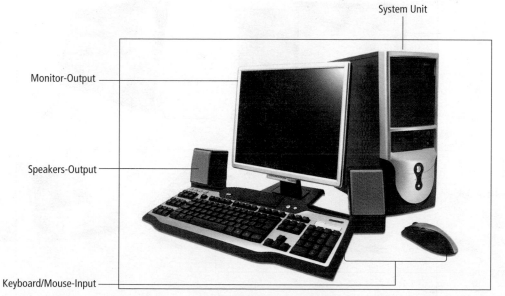

Figure 4 The components of a typical computer system and the appropriate step in the information processing cycle.

meaningful way. Think of data as the pieces of a jigsaw puzzle and information as the finished puzzle. Putting the pieces of the puzzle together gives you the overall picture. For example, CIS110, the letter B, and the name Amy Stevens are pieces of data. Individually, these pieces of data seem meaningless. However, when processed, this data becomes the information on a grade report that indicates Amy Stevens received a grade of B in her CIS 110 class.

These four basic computer functions work in a cycle known as the *information processing cycle* as shown in **Figure 3**.

The functions of this cycle are:

- *Input*—The computer gathers data or enables a user to enter data.

- *Process*—Data is manipulated and converted into information.

- *Output*—Information is displayed to the user in a way that is understandable.

- *Storage*—Data and/or information is stored for future use.

In the grade report, the instructor used a computer to enter, or input, the students' grades into the computerized grading system. A computer then processed this data along with data for other classes the students might have taken. In the example, the student Amy then received a record of her grade. The grade report was output by the computer. In addition, her grades remain stored in the system so they can be used to generate her transcript or to determine her future grade point average. See **Figure 4**.

Done! You have completed Objective 1 of 6.

► Computers have the same basic components; however, they vary in shape and size.

► Other computers include *mainframe computers, supercomputers,* and *embedded computers* and all vary in the tasks they perform.

What are the different types of computers and what are their uses? Although computers come in a variety of sizes, the basic components required to complete the information processing cycle must be present. In addition to microcomputers, there are specialty computers, including servers, mainframes, supercomputers, and embedded computers.

What are microcomputers? The term *microcomputer* means the main component of a computer is a microprocessor, a powerful chip that is very small in size compared to a mainframe or a supercomputer. Microcomputers are classified as small, inexpensive, and designed for personal use or as part of a network of computers in a business environment. As shown in **Figure 5**, some of the most common types of microcomputers include:

■ *Desktop computers* are computers that sit on the desk, floor, or table as shown in **Figure 6**. These computers typically have a detachable keyboard, mouse, monitor, and possibly other peripheral devices, such as digital cameras, scanners, and music players.

■ **Continue to the next page to complete the objective.** ➤

Microcomputer	Description
Desktop computer	A computer that sits on the desk, floor, or table and has peripheral devices such as a keyboard, mouse, and/or printer.
Gaming computer	A computer that is configured with a fast central processing unit, large amount of memory, a special video card, and joystick.
Notebook computer	A portable computer with a built-in screen, keyboard, and mouse.
Tablet computer	A portable computer has special features such as an onscreen keyboard.
Mobile devices	Personal digital assistants, handheld computers, and smartphones that are ultra-light and portable.

Figure 5   Most common types of microcomputers.

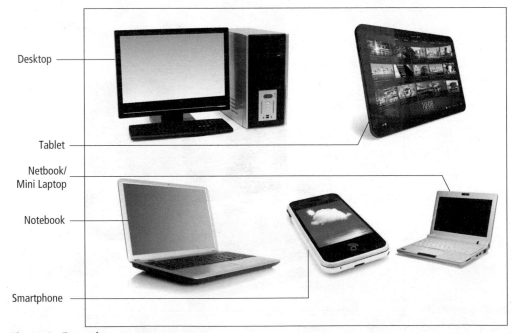

Desktop

Tablet

Netbook/ Mini Laptop

Notebook

Smartphone

Figure 6   Types of microcomputers.

Figure 7 An example of a desktop computer.

Figure 8 An example of a joystick used to control games.

- **Desktop computers,** as shown in **Figure 7,** are used in most homes and in business applications where portability is not needed. They can be configured in a multitude of arrangements depending on the specific needs and budget constraints. To *configure* means to put together by selecting a specific combination of components, features, and options.

- *Gaming computers* are mostly used by video game enthusiasts. They are usually configured with a fast CPU, large amount of memory, a special video card, a *joystick* as shown in **Figure 8,** or game pad, and sound card with surround sound speaker system.

Desktop computers generally fall into two main categories: PCs or Macs. The PC, or personal computer, originally referred to as the IBM personal computer when it was released in the early 1980s, is now manufactured by a variety of companies including Hewlett-Packard, Dell, and Gateway. The term *PC* commonly refers to a small microprocessor-based computer that typically runs a Windows operating system; however Macintosh computers are also known as personal computers. The Apple Macintosh computer, commonly known as Mac, is manufactured exclusively by Apple Inc. with an Intel microprocessor and can perform the same functions as the PC. The primary difference, then, between a personal computer and a Mac is the operating system as well as the user interface, application software and the cost of the computer.

There are pros and cons to both types of computers, but in reality, both are good systems and the choice usually comes down to personal preference and price. Although the PC and the Mac

■ **Continue to the next page to complete the objective.**

each process information differently, both can perform the same types of tasks. The PC has a larger market share among general computer users and in business settings, whereas the Mac is popular with graphic design, advertising, and professional audio and film industries.

Notebook computers, as shown in **Figure 9**, are ideal for people "on-the-go." Often referred to as laptops, they are equipped with rechargeable batteries and are designed to be portable. Notebooks typically have a built-in display screen, a keyboard, and a pointing device; although it is possible to connect them to detachable devices for more comfortable desktop use. A *docking station* enables the user to connect a notebook to a full-size keyboard, monitor, and other devices in an office setting.

Tablet computers are similar to notebooks because they are portable; however, they have some special features that set them apart.

Some tablet computers have a convertible touch screen that swivels, enabling the tablet to be used like a standard notebook computer in one position or like a clipboard in the second position. Information is typically typed into the tablet computer using an onscreen keyboard, as shown in **Figure 10**; the keyboard appears on the screen as opposed to a physical keyboard that sits on a desk.

■ **Continue to the next page to complete the objective.** ➡

Figure 9 Primary differences between a personal computer and a Macintosh computer include user interface, application software, and the cost and availability of parts and accessories.

Figure 10 A tablet.

Figure 11 Smartphones allow access to personal productivity software as well as Internet access.

Figure 12 Handhelds allow users to play music and take photos, for example.

Some also use **_speech-recognition_** technology, which enables the user to record discussions or lectures, or to control the computer functions using voice commands.

Mobile devices include items such as **_handheld computers_** (Pocket PCs), and **_smartphones_**. These devices vary in size and purpose, but they are all ultra-lightweight and portable. Handheld computers enable users to access personal productivity software and send email over the Internet. Smartphones, as shown in **Figure 11**, add Internet capability to the wireless communication aspects of cell phones. The Blackberry, iPhone, and Android are all examples of smartphones.

The newest mobile devices, often referred to simply as "handhelds," include personal productivity software and enable the user to play music, take photos and videos, make phone calls, and access the Internet as shown in **Figure 12**. As the features of mobile devices continue to converge, permitting them to perform similar tasks, it becomes more difficult to differentiate between them. If you are in the process of buying one of these handhelds, you need to do some research and make sure that you get the features and functions you want.

■ **Continue to the next page to complete the Objectives.**

Servers

What are servers? When computers are connected together in a *network* environment, *servers,* as shown in **Figure 13,** are specialized computers that manage network resources through the use of administrative software. They provide other computers with access to the network and can handle a variety of functions or may be assigned to just one particular type of task. Thus, within the same company, you might find a web server that holds and delivers the organization's web pages, a file server that handles the storage and retrieval tasks for all of the company's files, and a printer server that handles all print requests.

What are mainframe computers? **Mainframe computers,** as shown in **Figure 14,** are large computers often found in large businesses, organizations, and government agencies where thousands of users need to simultaneously use the data and resources of their institution such as in bulk data processing or when you use an automated teller machine to interact with your bank. Mainframes can store vast amounts of data using a variety of storage. Mainframes are often used for high-security applications, bulk data processing such as data surveys and censuses, and statistics. Early mainframe computers were very large and required separate rooms to house them, while today's mainframes are significantly smaller, faster, and more powerful than their predecessors. Today, mainframes are giving way to cloud computing. **Cloud computing**, in its simplest form, is the use of resources and applications which are accessible through a network connection to the Internet. These applications are housed on the Internet in a "cloud" and are

■ **Continue to the next page to complete the Objectives.** ➤

Figure 13 Network server.

Figure 14 Mainframe computer.

Figure 15 A close up image of a supercomputer.

In Automobiles...	In Appliances...
• Emission control systems	• Electronic appliances
• Antilock braking systems (ABS)	• Microwave ovens
• Airbags	• Digital cameras
• Stability control systems	• Programmable thermostats
	• Medical devices
	• Diagnostic equipment

Figure 16 Examples of embedded computers.

then accessed through a laptop or some other computing device with an Internet connection as opposed to installing the application on the laptop directly.

Supercomputers

What are supercomputers? Supercomputers are large, powerful, and ultrafast computers that perform specialized tasks. Some of these are used for research at a university, processing intensive scientific calculations like at NASA, and multi-scale simulations, for example. Since June 2008, the IBM nicknamed "Roadrunner," at the Department of Energy's Los Alamos National Laboratory in New Mexico, holds the top spot as the world's fastest supercomputer. (See http://www.top500.org/ for more information.)

Supercomputers, as shown in **Figure 15**, are the fastest and most expensive computers. Unlike a mainframe computer that can handle a number of programs simultaneously, the supercomputer is designed to run fewer programs at one time, but to do so as quickly as possible. They perform sophisticated mathematical calculations, track weather patterns, monitor satellites, and perform other complex tasks.

Embedded Computers

What are embedded computers? Embedded computers are small specialized computers built into larger components such as automobiles and appliances as demonstrated in the table in **Figure 16**. These computers use a specially programmed microprocessor to perform a set of predefined tasks, and may require little or no input from the user.

Done! You have completed Objective 2 of 6.

▶ **Hardware** is the computer and any equipment connected to it such as input devices, keyboards, the mouse, output devices, and monitors.

▶ Hardware also consists of the system unit, which includes the **motherboard** and the **central processing unit (CPU)**.

What is computer hardware? Hardware devices are the physical components of the computer. Items such as the monitor, keyboard, mouse, and printer as shown in Figure 4 are also known as **peripherals** because they attach to the computer.

The computer itself is known as the **system unit,** and it contains many of the critical hardware and electrical components. The system unit is sometimes referred to as the tower, box, or console. When the system unit is combined with the appropriate peripheral devices, the system can perform the four basic computer functions: input, process, output, and storage. Peripheral devices are used to input and output data and information, and the system unit processes and stores the data.

System Unit

What is inside the system unit? If you remove the cover from the system unit, you will find several key components inside. One of the most essential components is the **motherboard,** a large printed circuit board, as shown in **Figure 17**, to which all the other components are connected.

The **microprocessor chip,** also known as the **central processing unit (CPU)** and RAM, the computer's main memory, are connected to the motherboard. The table in **Figure 18** lists the motherboard features and their descriptions.

■ **Continue to the next page to complete the objective.**

Processor socket (CPU)

Memory modules (RAM)

Expansion slots

Motherboard

Figure 17 The motherboard and some of its components.

Component	Description
Motherboard/System board	The main computer circuit board into which all components are plugged. It is installed safely inside the box or case called the system unit.
CPU	The central processing unit is responsible for getting data from memory, performing arithmetic and logical operations and converting data to information.
Memory modules (RAM)	Temporary storage area where data is stored before processing, output, or storage. RAM is the center of flow of data and information within the information processing cycle.
Expansion slots	Slots or connectors on the motherboard that allow you to connect expansion cards.
Expansion cards	Removable circuit boards used to add new peripherals or increase the computer's capabilities. If the motherboard does not have a specific port to connect a peripheral device, the appropriate expansion card will allow you to do so.
Ports	Connecting points used as an interface between peripherals and the motherboard.

Figure 18 Motherboard features.

Keyboard

Figure 19 Examples of input devices.

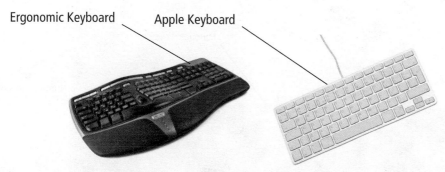

Ergonomic Keyboard   Apple Keyboard

Figure 20 Examples of keyboards.

The motherboard also provides some of the ports used to connect peripheral devices, which are explained later in this chapter to the system.

Input Devices

Input devices are used to enter data into memory (RAM) and are the primary way we interface with a computer. Some of the common input devices are the keyboard and the mouse as shown in **Figure 19**.

Keyboards

Are there different types of keyboards? The **keyboard** is the primary input device for computers. There are actually several different kinds of keyboards; a small sample is shown in **Figure 20**. The QWERTY keyboard is the most common. It is based on the original typewriter keyboard and is named for the arrangement of the letters on the upper left alphabetic row of keys. Another style is the Dvorak keyboard, which arranges the letters and numbers in a different pattern for increased typing speed. Some ergonomic keyboards use a split keyboard arrangement, offsetting each half at an angle to reduce the incidence of repetitive stress injuries such as carpal tunnel syndrome. The onscreen keyboard, as found on the iPad, supplies the actual keyboard on the actual screen. This type of keyboard, along with smartphone keyboards are not only changing the way we type but are also a more desirable alternative for those who tend to be more mobile.

Keyboard size and layout on notebook and tablet computers can differ slightly from a standard keyboard due to space constraints. Keyboards usually send information to the computer through a cable connected to a USB

■ **Continue to the next page to complete the objective.**

port; however, *wireless* or remote keyboards are gaining in popularity. A wireless keyboard communicates with the computer by infrared or radio frequency technology. These wireless devices require batteries.

What are all these other keys used for? In addition to the standard keys originally found on typewriters, computer keyboards have a variety of keys that provide additional functionality.

Control keys, such as the Ctrl, Alt, and Cmd keys (the Cmd key is typically only found on Mac computers), provide shortcuts or increased functionality to the keyboard when used in combination with another key as listed in the table in **Figure 21**. If you press the Shift key and a letter, the result is an uppercase letter. In the same way, using one of the control keys enables the standard keys to be used for additional purposes. For example, pressing Ctrl and the letter P opens the Print dialog box. Another example of a control key is the Esc key, which can often be used to stop, or *escape,* from a currently running task. A unique control key that is found only on Windows-based keyboards is the Windows key; when pressed alone, it serves as a shortcut key to open the Start menu, and when pressed in combination with other keys, it opens many common functions through the keyboard.

The ***numeric keypad,*** located at the right of the keyboard, provides an alternative method of quickly entering numbers. This is useful for individuals who are accustomed to using an adding machine or calculator.

Function keys are located above the standard row of number keys as shown in **Figure 22**. Numbered F1 through F12, these keys are generally associated with certain software-specific commands. Pressing the F1 key will usually

■ **Continue to the next page to complete the objective.**

Windows Shortcut	Mac Shortcut	Command
Ctrl-O	Cmd-A	Select All
Ctrl-P	Cmd-P	Print
Ctrl-O	Cmd-O	Open
Ctrl-N	Cmd-N	New (window, document)
Ctrl-S	Cmd-S	Save
Ctrl-C	Cmd-C	Copy
Ctrl-X	Cmd-X	Cut
Ctrl-V	Cmd-V	Paste
Ctrl-W	Cmd-W	Close Window
Ctrl-B	Cmd-B	Bold (selected text)
Ctrl-I	Cmd-I	Italic (selected text)

Figure 21   Keystroke shortcuts.

Figure 22   The function keys are generally associated with software-specific commands.

Toggle Keys

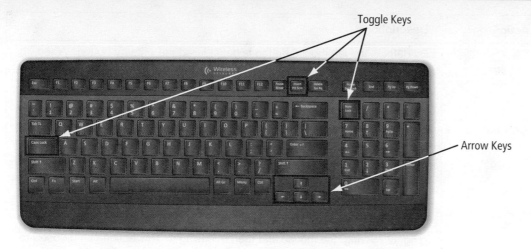

Arrow Keys

Figure 23 The arrow keys allow users to move the insertion point while the toggle keys are used for various purposes.

open the Help menu for a program; however, pressing one of the other function keys can produce different results, depending on the software program running.

Arrow keys are located at the bottom of the keyboard between the standard keys and the numeric keypad as shown in **Figure 23**. These keys enable the user to move the insertion point around the window one space at a time.

Toggle and other keys are used for various purposes, including navigation and editing. The Insert, Num Lock, and Caps Lock keys are all examples of toggle keys. A *toggle key* works just like a light switch; press it once and the feature is turned on, press it again and it is turned off. If you've ever accidentally pressed the Caps Lock key and typed a long string of all capital letters, you've seen this feature in action. Pressing the Caps Lock key again allows you to return to normal keyboarding mode.

Multimedia and Internet control keys are typically found at the top edge of the keyboard. The precise placement and function of these keys usually depends on the keyboard manufacturer. However, most modern keyboards have at least a few keys or buttons that can be used for such tasks as muting or adjusting speaker volume, opening a *web browser*, and sending an email. Generally, each button has an *icon* that indicates its function.

The Mouse

Is there an easier way to control the action on the computer screen? Yes, the *mouse,* as shown in **Figure 24**, is an input device (also called a

Figure 24 A mouse is an input device that allows the user to control the computer's operations.

■ **Continue to the next page to complete the objective.**

pointing device) that, together with the keyboard, enables the user to control the operations of the computer. The mouse became popular with the introduction of graphical user interfaces, such as Microsoft Windows. This point-and-click device is useful for positioning the *insertion point* by translating hand movements into corresponding actions on the screen. The mouse is represented on the screen by a symbol called the *mouse pointer*. The user moves the mouse and positions this pointer anywhere on the screen to move objects or make selections from available program icons or menus.

Some mice have a roller ball on the bottom that, as you move it, translates your movement into electrical impulses. Others use laser technology (optical) to control the pointer movement. Because the bottom of an optical mouse is sealed, dirt and debris are less likely to get inside and interfere with the mouse's internal mechanisms. Just like a keyboard, the mouse can be wired or wireless.

Notebook and tablet computers can use a mouse, but most of them have a built-in touchscreen, touchpad, a trackball, or track point to move the insertion point and mouse pointer. Most mice today are equipped with two buttons and a wheel button in the center that provides easy zoom and scroll functions.

How can the mouse be used more efficiently? Although there are different kinds of mice, the traditional mouse has two buttons and a scroll wheel. The table in **Figure 25** provides a brief description of some of the ways the mouse can be used.

■ **Continue to the next page to complete the objective.**

Action	Description
Click	By default, the left mouse button is considered the primary button. When instructed to click, it is understood that the mouse pointer is moved to a certain location on the screen, and the left mouse button is pressed and released one time.
Double-click	When instructed to double-click, it is understood that the mouse pointer is moved to a certain location on the screen and the left mouse button is pressed and released twice in rapid succession. It is important that the mouse does not move while double-clicking or the command will not produce the expected results.
Drag	This means to press the left mouse button and continue to hold it while dragging, or moving, the mouse and then releasing it. This action can be used to select large blocks of text, to move objects, or to resize other objects.
Right-click	Pressing and releasing the right mouse button one time will open a **Shortcut menu.** Shortcut menus are usually context-sensitive, which means they will vary depending on what or where you have clicked and what program you are using. The right mouse button is also known as the secondary button and is not typically pressed more than one time. After the shortcut menu has been opened, you select the appropriate choice by clicking it with the left mouse button.
Right-drag	This is done by pressing the right mouse button and continuing to hold it while dragging, or moving, the mouse. This action is used when copying or moving files or folders within different storage devices.
Scroll wheel	If your mouse is equipped with a scroll wheel (a scroll wheel can also be a clickable button), it can be used to quickly move a page up or down in a window, thus the name of the action to . It is an easy way to navigate through lengthy documents or websites.

Figure 25 Mouse functions.

Figure 26 An example of a CPU.

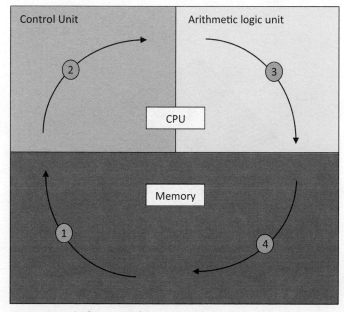

Figure 27 The four steps of the machine cycle are the same in all systems, from personal computers to mainframes. What differs is the speed at which the cycle is performed.

Are there other input devices? Although the keyboard and mouse are the two most common input devices, there are many other input devices. *Scanners* are similar to copy machines, but instead of producing a paper copy, they convert documents or photos to digital files that can then be saved on your computer.

The Processor

What does the CPU do? The CPU, as shown in **Figure 26**, is the brain of the computer and is responsible for executing program instructions and manipulating data to convert to information. It has two main parts—the *control unit* and the *arithmetic logic unit (ALU)* as shown in **Figure 27**. The control unit is responsible for obtaining and executing instructions from the computer's memory. Example: The user wants to print a document and selects the "Print" command from an icon on the screen. The CPU gets the command from memory (RAM), interprets the command, and sends the document as output to a selected printer. In other words, the CPU coordinates the internal activities and the activities of all the other computer components.

The arithmetic logic unit (ALU) performs the arithmetic and logic functions for the computer. The ALU handles addition, subtraction, multiplication, and division and also makes logical and comparison decisions. This enables the CPU to perform tasks such as sorting data alphabetically or numerically and filtering data to locate specific criteria.

■ **Continue to the next page to complete the objective.**

Different CPUs

As important as the CPU is to your computer, you might expect it to take up a large amount of space in the console. However, a CPU is actually rather small, thus the term *microchip*. Over the years, manufacturers have reduced the size of microprocessor chips while continuing to increase their computing power.

In fact, Moore's law (formulated in 1965 by Gordon Moore, cofounder of Intel) addresses this increase in computing power, as shown in **Figure 28**, observing that current production methods enable CPU capacity to double about every 24 months or so!

Are there different brands of CPUs? Yes, the most well-known chip manufacturers include Intel and Advanced Micro Devices (AMD). Chip manufacturers often produce several different models of chips. Some of the chips that Intel makes include the *Intel® Core™ i7 processor Extreme Edition,* the *Intel Core™2 Quad Processor* for desktops, and the *Intel Centrino® 2 Processor Technology* for portable computers. AMD manufactures chips such as the *AMD Phenom™ II X4* for desktops, and the *AMD Turion™ X2 Ultra Dual-Core Mobile Processor* for portable computers. Intel and AMD chips are the mainstays for PCs. Using multiple processors (***dual core*** or quad core) has several advantages over a single-processor CPU as shown in **Figure 29**, including improved multitasking capabilities and system performance, lower power consumption, reduced usage of system resources, and lower heat emissions.

■ **Continue to the next page to complete the objective.**

Figure 28   Moore's Law graphically represented.

Figure 29   A single-core CPU can handle multiple applications by rapidly switching between applications. A multicore CPU can (with the right software) divide the work load between processors, assigning multiple cores to labor-intensive tasks such as photo or video editing.

Early processors	Processed at speeds of less than 5 MHz
Modern processors	Operate at over 3 GHz (equivalent of 3,000 MHz)
Newer processors	Continue to surpass 3 GHz

Figure 30 CPU processors.

Figure 31 Random Access Memory (RAM)/RAM chips.

How is a CPU's processing power measured? One indicator of a CPU's processing power is its **clock speed,** which measures the speed at which a CPU processes data and is measured in **megahertz (MHz)** or **gigahertz (GHz),** depending on the age of the CPU. **Figure 30** displays various processors and their speeds. However, looking at clock speed is not always the best indicator. Instead, how many millions of instructions processed per second, or MIPS, is a better measurement. These instructions can also be measured in billions, and trillions of instructions per second (BIPS and TIPS).

What types of memory does a computer have? Memory is another computer component of a computer system. The term *memory* signifies storage. There are two basic types of memory: temporary or **volatile** and permanent or **nonvolatile.**

Permanent memory includes **Read-Only Memory (ROM),** which is prerecorded on a chip. The information on a ROM chip cannot be changed, removed, or rewritten and is generally inaccessible to the computer user. ROM is nonvolatile memory because it retains its contents even if the computer is turned off. ROM contains critical information, such as the program used to start up or boot the computer.

Storage devices such as hard disks and flash drives and storage media such as CDs and DVDs are considered permanent or nonvolatile memory and are presented later in this chapter.

Temporary memory, the computer's temporary or volatile memory, is **Random Access Memory (RAM).** RAM, as shown in **Figure 31**, acts as the computer's short-term memory and stores data and program instructions waiting

■ **Continue to the next page to complete the objective.** ➤

to be processed. RAM is considered volatile because its contents are erased when the computer is turned off.

Why is it important to have enough RAM? The more tasks your computer performs at the same time, or the more programs you have open, the more RAM it uses. We described RAM earlier as the center of the flow of data and information in the information-processing cycle as shown in **Figure 32**. That flow slows down when there is not enough RAM. Your computer's RAM is like the top of your desk. The size of the desk that you need is determined by the work you do at a given moment. You may need to use a notebook computer, several books, a clipboard with notes, a holder for pens and pencils, and a telephone. If your desk is not big enough to fit these items, you cannot work with all of them at the same time. If you do not have a sufficient amount of RAM in your system, you might notice your computer slows down or even stops responding when you try to perform tasks.

Computer users often think this means they have too much information saved on their computers' hard drives. What it actually means is that they are running out of memory, not permanent storage space. To fix this problem, you can reduce the number of programs running at the same time, disable some features of the operating system, or simply add more RAM to your system as shown in **Figure 33**. Installing additional memory is one of the most inexpensive and easiest upgrades for your computer and often results in noticeable performance improvements.

■ **Continue to the next page to complete the objective.**

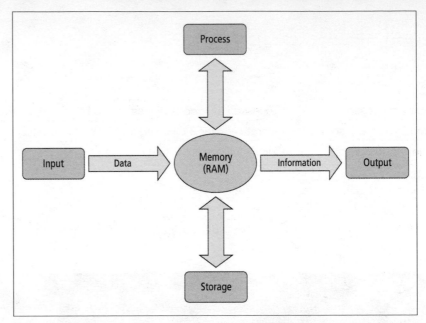

Figure 32 These are the four computer functions within the information processing cycle. Memory is not considered a function, but it is the center of flow of data and information within this cycle.

Figure 33 Adding RAM to a computer is quite simple and relatively inexpensive.

Units to Measure Memory

Name	Abbreviation	Number of Bytes	Relative Size
Byte	**B**	1 byte	Holds one character of data
Kilobyte	**KB**	1,024 bytes	Holds about a half page of double-spaced text
Megabyte	**MB**	1,048,576 bytes	Holds about 768 pages of typed text
Gigabyte	**GB**	1,073,741,824 bytes	Holds approximately 786,432 pages of text
Terabyte	**TB**	1,099,511,627,776 bytes	This represents a stack of typewritten pages almost 51 miles high
Petabyte	**PB**	1,125,899,906,842,624 bytes	This represents a stack of typewritten pages almost 52,000 miles high

Figure 34 Measuring memory—these units are used to measure the size and capacity of RAM and also of storage devices/media.

Figure 35 Output devices—monitors.

Memory is measured in several units such as *megabytes (MB),* which is approximately one million bytes, *gigabytes (GB),* which is approximately one billion bytes, or *terabytes (TR),* which is one trillion bytes. The table in **Figure 34** displays some of the units of memory and their relative size.

RAM size requirements vary depending on the operating system in use. Older computers that run Windows XP should have between 512 MB to 1 GB of RAM. For newer computers, a minimum of 2 GB possibly more is recommended.

Output Devices

Output devices display information after data has been processed in a useful format. This format can be text, graphics, audio, or video. Monitors and printers are the two most common output devices.

Monitors

What are monitors? A monitor, as shown in **Figure 35**, is a display devices that shows images of text, graphics, and video once data has been processed. The image on a monitor is called *soft copy*; you can view it, but you cannot touch it.

What is an LCD monitor? Monitors come in a variety of sizes and styles, but the standard today is the *LCD (liquid crystal display).* *Flat-panel* LCD monitors use a liquid crystal display and are thin and energy efficient.

What factors determine a monitor's display quality? The number of *pixels,* a monitor's display, is made up of millions of tiny dots known as pixels or picture element. Each pixel represents a single point on a display screen or in a graphic image.

■ **Continue to the next page to complete the objective.**

The number of pixels on the screen determines a monitor's sharpness and clarity, also known as *resolution,* as shown in **Figure 36.** A higher number of pixels results in a clearer and sharper monitor resolution. A standard screen resolution might be expressed as 1024 x 768, which means there are 1,024 columns, each containing 768 pixels, for a total of more than 786,000 pixels on the screen. Monitor sizes are determined by measuring their screens diagonally.

Dot pitch is another display characteristic and refers to the diagonal distance between two pixels of the same color. Dot pitch is measured in millimeters with smaller measurements resulting in a crisper viewing image because there is less blank space between the pixels. For best viewing, monitors should have a dot pitch measurement of .28 mm or less. LCD monitors use an electric current to illuminate the pixels.

Refresh rate is the speed at which the pixels are illuminated, and it's measured in cycles per second, expressed as hertz (Hz). Refresh rates generally average between 75 and 85 Hz, which means the screen image is redrawn 75 to 85 times per second. Higher refresh rates result in less screen flicker and less eye strain.

What are touch screen monitors? Touch screen monitors are both input and output devices. They display images just like regular monitors but also enable users to touch their surfaces and make selections directly from the screen as shown in **Figure 37.**

■ **Continue to the next page to complete the objective.** ▶

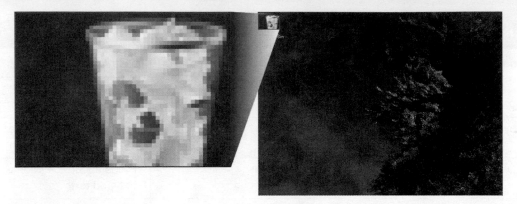

Figure 36 An image on a computer display is made up of rows of tiny colored pixels. A monitor's image is refreshed many times per second; with each refresh, the color displayed by each pixel might change.

Figure 37 A touch screen monitor.

These monitors are widely used in retail stores at checkout counters, in airports for passengers' fast check-ins, and HP has released a personal computer in which the monitor is also the system unit and uses *touch screen technology*.

Which monitor is best? Choosing the right monitor is always a combination of what you like, want, and can afford. A higher resolution, small dot pitch, fast refresh rate, and large monitor size are desirable, but all come with a higher price tag.

Printers

Using a monitor is a good way to view the information on your computer, but sometimes a soft copy isn't sufficient for your needs. *Printers* generate a *hard copies* or *printouts,* which are a permanent record of your work on paper.

What types of printers are available? There are two categories of printers: impact and nonimpact. *Impact* printers have small hammers, similar to a typewriter's, that strike an ink ribbon against paper as shown on the right in **Figure 38**, leaving behind the image of the character or symbol. The *dot matrix* printer as shown on the left in **Figure 38** is also an impact printer. Once very popular because of their low cost, dot matrix printers are still in use today, limited only to certain applications that require continuous forms or multipart forms (an original and several copies), such as invoices or purchase orders.

How does a nonimpact printer work? *Nonimpact* printers, as shown in **Figure 39**, do not actually touch the paper when printing. There are varieties of nonimpact printers,

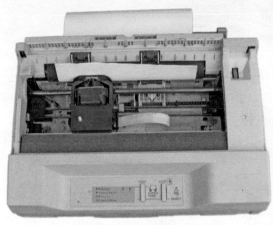

Figure 38 A dot matrix printer (left) and a typewriter (right) are both impact printers.

Figure 39 Inkjet printers are popular among home users, especially with the rise of digital photography.

■ **Continue to the next page to complete the objective.**

but the two most commonly used with home computers are the ink-jet printer and the laser printer.

The *inkjet* printer uses a special nozzle and ink cartridges to spray ink in small droplets onto the paper. Inkjet printers easily print in color, in black, and in grayscale to produce good quality printouts. They are relatively inexpensive to buy and maintain.

Laser printers, as shown in **Figure 40,** use a special cylinder known as a drum, dry ink or toner, and a laser. Static electricity attracts toner to the surface of the drum, and the laser distributes the toner in the correct pattern. The drum transfers the toner to the paper, and heat is used to permanently fuse the toner to the paper. Laser printers are generally more expensive to purchase than inkjet printers, although they often print more quickly and are more cost effective. Lower-end laser printers print only in black and white; however, more expensive printers can produce color copies.

How do you assess a printer's capabilities? When you select a printer, there are some key characteristics to consider.

Print speed is often expressed as *pages per minute* (*ppm*). Print speed can vary depending on the manufacturer and model, as well as printer type and is also affected by whether the page is text-only, if it includes graphics, and if the printout is in color or in black and grayscale. **Figure 41** shows a relatively fast laser printer as compared to an inkjet printer, for example, as it has higher ppms.

■ **Continue to the next page to complete the objective.** ▶

Figure 40   Output devices—a laser printer.

Figure 41   Laser printers print quickly and offer high-quality printouts.

All-in-one devices usually include:

- A printer, either inkjet (color or black and grayscale) or laser (output)

- A scanner to convert text or images into files that can be stored and further manipulated by the computer (input)

- A facsimile (fax) function to send and receive documents via

- the telephone (communications)

- A copier function to duplicate documents (output)

- Network capabilities to enable this multifunction device (MFD) to work as part of a network environment both wired or wireless (communications)

Figure 42   What are all-in-one printers?

Figure 43   Projectors are output devices which allow information to be displayed on a big screen for many to view.

Just as with monitors, resolution is also important to print quality. For printing purposes, resolution is expressed as *dots per inch* or *dpi*. The higher the dpi, the better the print quality. Print qualities of 300 to 600 dpi are typical of most printers, although special photo printers can offer resolutions up to 1,200 dpi. Professional printers can reach even higher values.

Color output and its related cost is another important consideration. Ink-jet printers offer four- or six-color options. Many ink-jet printers use one cartridge for black ink and one or more cartridges for color. When available, printers that offer a separate cartridge for each color are a practical choice because you need to replace only one color at a time as the cartridges run out. Laser printers use separate toner cartridges for each color.

Some printers are considered all-in-one-printers and bundle multiple capabilities into one device as listed in **Figure 42**.

Speakers and Multimedia Projectors

Are there other output devices? Speakers and *multimedia projectors,* as shown in **Figure 43**, are also examples of output devices. Many computers include small speakers to enable the user to listen to CDs or DVDs and hear any auditory signals the computer sends. However, if you're serious about multimedia, you will probably want to invest in a better set of speakers for improved performance. Multimedia projectors are used to conduct presentations and training sessions. These projectors enable information to be displayed on a big screen so it can be easily viewed by a large group of attendees.

■ Continue to the next page to complete the objectives.

Under what category do digital cameras fall? A digital camera is a device that stores pictures digitally rather than using conventional film. After images are captured, they are stored in the camera's internal memory. Some cameras use removable flash memory cards as storage media. These cards can be read by a computer, which can then edit them and save them as files. So, the camera itself is a form of "handheld" computer, which, if connected to a computer, serves as an input/output device. The same thing can describe camcorders.

Storage Devices

What are storage devices? Storage devices are used to store the data, information, and programs for future use. This storage is often referred to as *permanent memory* because, unlike data that is in RAM, data saved to a storage device remains there until the user deletes or overwrites it. Data can be stored using internal hardware devices located in the system unit or in removable units that enable portability. See **Figure 44**.

How is a storage device different than storage media? A *storage device* is a piece of hardware such as a hard drive or a DVD drive. Media is the removable part that actually contains the stored data. Media requires a device to *read* and *write* on it. Read is the action of retrieving or opening existing data and write is the action of saving or storing data. See **Figure 45** for a list of devices and their media.

■ **Continue to the next page to complete the objective.** ➤

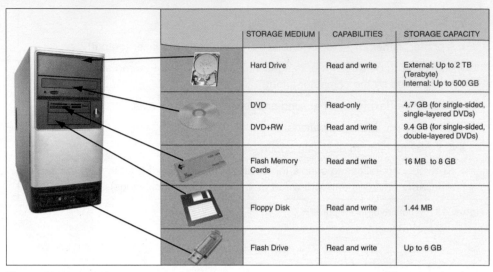

	STORAGE MEDIUM	CAPABILITIES	STORAGE CAPACITY
	Hard Drive	Read and write	External: Up to 2 TB (Terabyte) Internal: Up to 500 GB
	DVD	Read-only	4.7 GB (for single-sided, single-layered DVDs)
	DVD+RW	Read and write	9.4 GB (for single-sided, double-layered DVDs)
	Flash Memory Cards	Read and write	16 MB to 8 GB
	Floppy Disk	Read and write	1.44 MB
	Flash Drive	Read and write	Up to 6 GB

Figure 44   Storage devices.

Device	Media
CD and DVD optical drives	Read and write on CDs and DVDs
Card readers	Read and write on flash memory cards
USB port	Read and write on flash drives or thumb drives
Tape backup drives	Read and write onto tape cartridges
The hard drive is the exception, in that the hardware and the media are all contained in a sealed unit that cannot be taken apart.	

Figure 45   A list of devices and their media.

Figure 46 Hard drives store data magnetically on metal platters. The platters are stacked, and read/write heads move across the surface of the platters, reading data and writing it to memory.

Figure 47 The data on an optical disc is read by a laser.

How is data stored? Data is generally stored using one of three forms of storage: magnetic, optical, or flash memory:

- *Magnetic* storage uses tape or film covered in a thin, magnetic coating that enables data to be saved as magnetic impulses. It works in much the same fashion as an audiocassette or videotape works. Hard drives and backup tape drives are both forms of magnetic storage as shown in **Figure 46**.

  Before magnetic storage can occur, media has to be formatted. This is the process in which media is divided into *tracks* and *sectors*. Tracks are magnetic concentric circles and sectors are segments within those circles. Data is stored magnetically within the spaces created by these tracks sectors. Magnetic media has read/write capability, which means it is possible to use it over and over again, enabling you to delete or revise existing data and save new data.

- *Optical* storage uses flat plastic discs coated in a special reflective material as shown in **Figure 47**. Data is saved by using a laser beam to burn tiny pits into the storage medium. A less intensive laser is used to read the saved data. The saved data is organized using sectors, similar to those used in magnetic media. *Compact discs (CDs)* and *digital video discs (DVDs)* are examples of optical media. Unlike magnetic media, not all optical storage is read/write capable. *CD-ROMs*—CD media that was burned once and from that moment on can only be read—and *DVD-ROMs*—

■ Continue to the next page to complete the objective.

DVD media that is burned once and from that moment on can only be read—are considered read-only media (ROM). The information contained on them can be read, but not changed or deleted, and it is not possible to save new data to them. If you purchase new software, music, or a movie, it is most likely on a DVD-ROM as shown in **Figure 48**.

A record-only disc (CD-R) enables you to record, or *burn,* information to the disc one time only; information saved this way cannot be deleted or rewritten. A rewritable disc (CD-RW) enables information to be recorded, revised, or deleted, and new data can also be written to the disc, similar to magnetic media. The same possibilities are available in DVDs. While there used to be two competing DVD formats, DVD – R/RW and DVD + R/RW, that were incompatible with one another, manufacturers have since replaced the two competing formats with drives that could read both and are called DVD + R. **Figure 49** summarizes the capabilities of these various formats.

What is LightScribe? LightScribe is a disc-labeling technology that burns text and graphics onto the surface of a specially coated LightScribe CD or DVD. This is an alternative to printing a conventional sticker label and attaching it to a regular CD or DVD but it does require that you purchase LightScribe media.

■ **Continue to the next page to complete the objective.**

Figure 48 The information contained on a DVD can be read, but not changed.

Format	Capabilities
CD-ROM	Information is recorded once and can only be read. Information cannot be changed or deleted; new information cannot be added.
CD-R	Record information to a disc one time. Information cannot be deleted or rewritten.
CD-RW	Information can be recorded, revised, or deleted; new data can be written to the disc.
DVD-ROM	Media is recorded once and can only be read. Information cannot be changed or deleted; new information cannot be added.
DVD±R/RW	Information can be recorded and rewritten.

Figure 49 CD and DVD formats.

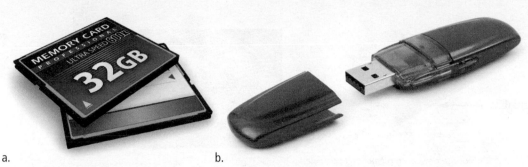

a. b.

Figure 50 Flash memory devices. a. An SD flash memory card is one of the most popular kinds of solid-state storage used in digital cameras and other digital media devices. b. A USB flash (thumb) drive can store gigabytes of data and plug into a computer's USB port.

Figure 51 Internal hard drives hold the data and instructions that the computer needs and are inaccessible from outside the system.

Flash memory, as shown in **Figure 50**, uses solid-state technology. It is completely electronic and has no moving mechanical parts. Flash memory is a quick and easy form of rewritable storage and is often used in mobile devices such as PDAs, digital cameras, and MP3 players. Depending on the manufacturer, flash memory cards may be called Memory Stick, CompactFlash, Secure Digital, or MultiMediaCard. Typically, a device can use only one style of memory card; however, a computer equipped with the appropriate card reader can read any of them. Small, removable storage devices known as flash drives or thumb drives also use flash technology, require a USB port to connect to the system unit, and are very popular to transport data.

What are the main types of storage devices? Depending on the age and type of computer you have, you might find some or all of the following internal storage options:

- *Hard disk drive*—shown in **Figure 51**, is the computer's main internal storage device. Also referred to as a hard drive, its storage space is usually measured in gigabytes (GB), with newer computers ranging in size from 80 GB to 750 GB, although it is possible to find some specialized, high-end computers with storage space measuring up to 2 terabytes (TB). As with everything else in computing, these numbers tend to increase with each new model. Hard drives are traditionally permanent storage devices fixed inside the system unit.

■ **Continue to the next page to complete the objective.**

- *Floppy disk drive*—This is a device that reads/writes *floppy diskettes* that have a maximum storage capacity of 1,450 MB. Because of this limited storage capacity, you will seldom see floppy disks used today.

- *CD and/or DVD drives*—Previously, computers contained either one or two of these optical drives in the system unit. Today, however, computers typically contain a drive that can read and/or write DVDs. It's important to know whether these drives are simple CD-ROM drives, which can only read CDs, or if it is a *CD-RW* drive, also known as a CD burner. A *CD burner* gives you the ability to save, or burn, files to a *CD-R* (compact disk recordable).

Although CDs and DVDs look alike, DVDs are capable of holding more information than CDs. A CD can hold up to 700 MB of data, but a DVD can store almost 10 GB! Because of their differences, a CD drive is unable to read DVDs, although a DVD drive can read CDs. **Figure 52** displays a some of the storage devices just discussed.

Is it possible to add a storage device to a system? If you are running out of hard disk space or your system doesn't have a particular storage device, it may be possible to add storage space, provided your system has enough room. You would need an available drive bay, which is the physical location within the system unit, or you might consider removing an existing device and replacing it with another as shown in **Figure 53**. For instance, if you only

■ **Continue to the next page to complete the objective.** ►

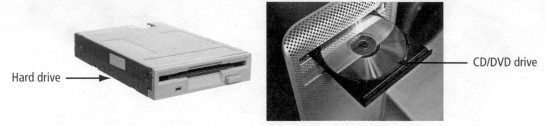

Hard drive ⟶   CD/DVD drive

Figure 52 Storage devices in a notebook computer.

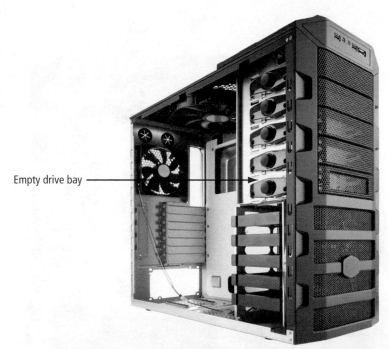

Empty drive bay ⟶

Figure 53 A desktop computer with an available drive bay for adding a storage device.

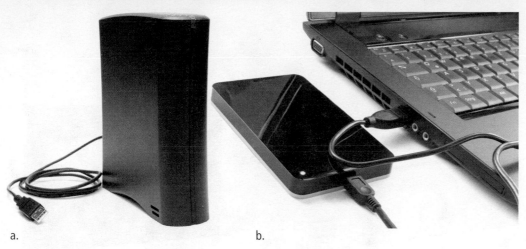

a.   b.

Figure 54   a. High capacity external hard drives are often used to back up data on internal hard drives. b. Smaller external hard drives enable you to take a significant amount of data on the road with you.

have a CD-ROM drive, you could remove that and replace it with a CD-RW/DVD drive, thereby giving you the ability to read and burn CDs and play DVDs too. It is also possible to purchase many of these units as external storage devices. An external storage device is a peripheral that attaches to the computer via a port and performs the same tasks as its corresponding internal device. One of the most popular is the external hard drive as shown in **Figure 54**, which can greatly increase a computer's storage capacity and make your data fully portable.

Are there other types of storage devices? Other storage devices you might be familiar with include flash drives, a currently popular form of data storage, and older but still reliable backup tape drives.

Flash drives are removable storage devices that use flash memory and connect to the computer by a USB port. Flash drives are also known as thumb drives, universal serial bus (USB) drives, and jump drives. The flash drive is typically a device small enough to fit on a keychain or in a pocket (as shown in **Figure 55**) and, because of its solid-state circuitry and lack of moving parts, is extremely durable. Available in several storage sizes ranging from 16 MB to 64 GB, a flash drive is a quick and easy way to save and transport files. As an example, a 128-MB flash drive, which is relatively small, holds the equivalent of almost 35 songs! To use one of these devices, you simply plug

Figure 55   Flash drives are a convenient means of portable storage and come in many different shapes and sizes.

■ **Continue to the next page to complete the objective.**

it into a computer's USB port. The computer recognizes the new device and enables the user to save or retrieve files from the flash drive.

Backup tape drives are storage devices that save data to magnetic tape media as shown in **Figure 56**. Although they are rarely used for home computers anymore, many businesses still rely on tape backup systems to safeguard data.

The capacity of the components found in your system unit is measured in terms of storage size or speed. Computer systems continue to increase in storage capacity and computing speed, while decreasing in size. Generally, higher measurements indicate a system that is quicker and more powerful than a system with lower measurements. However, it is important to balance size and speed with financial considerations too.

Although it is tempting to consider buying a computer with the most power possible, a lesser computer may be more reasonably priced and still be sufficient for your needs. Recall CPU speeds are measured in gigahertz (GHz). The amount of RAM in a computer is generally measured in gigabytes (GB) and terabytes (TB) while storage space is usually measured in megabytes or gigabytes (GB), depending on the device.

Figure 56   Tape backup drive and media.

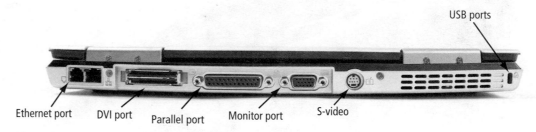

Figure 57   Ports.

Ports

What are ports? A ***port*** acts as an interface or connector between a system's peripheral devices and the computer, enabling data to be exchanged easily. Ports have different shapes and sizes as shown in **Figure 57**.

■ **Continue to the next page to complete the objective.** ▶

Various input and output devices use different data exchange methods, requiring different types of ports and connectors (or plugs) as shown in **Figure 58**. If your computer does not have a particular port, you can buy an expansion card that connects to the motherboard and provides the needed connection.

How do you determine which port a peripheral device needs? Manufacturers have attempted to make the process of connecting peripheral devices less complicated on newer computers. Rather than trying to match the size and shape of a connector to its port, many manufacturers now use a color-coding system that coordinates the colors of the connectors with their corresponding ports. Additionally, many newer desktop computers include ports, such as USB and audio ports as shown in **Figure 59**. Positioning these ports on the front or side panels makes it a simple process to connect and disconnect devices that are used only occasionally, such as digital cameras, external hard drives, or MP3 players. Peripherals that are rarely disconnected, such as a keyboard or printer, are generally plugged into the ports on the back of the computer.

What are the different ports used for? Serial and parallel ports are two of the oldest types of

■ **Continue to the next page to complete the objective.**

Figure 58 A motherboard contains slots for expansion cards.

USB port

Audio port

Figure 59 Examples of a USB and an audio port.

ports found on a computer. *Serial ports* send data one bit at a time, so the data exchange rate is slow compared to newer technology.

The maximum rate at which a standard serial port can transfer data is 115 *kilobits* or one thousand bits per second (Kbps). The mouse and modem are examples of devices that might use a serial port. A *parallel port,* as shown in **Figure 60**, sends data in groups of bits, at transfer rates of up to 500 Kbps, so it is a considerably faster method of transferring data than the serial port.

Are there faster ports? Over the years, newer ports have come into existence. One of these is the *universal serial bus (USB) port,* as shown in **Figure 61**, which is able to interface with several different peripheral devices, reducing the need for individual, dedicated ports. USB ports are also able to transfer data at extremely high rates of speed. Original USB ports, known as USB 1.1, are capable of speeds of 12 *megabits* or one million bits per second (Mbps). The newest version, USB 3.0, can attain a rate of 5 Gbps, 10 times faster than USB 2.0 technology. USB 3.0 ports are backward compatible, which means that older USB devices work with them. The higher data transfer capabilities of USB ports, coupled with their capability to work with multiple devices,

■ **Continue to the next page to complete the objective.** ►

Parallel port

Figure 60   Example of a parallel port.

Figure 61   A USB port and a USB connector.

Port Name	Data Transfer Speed	Typical Use
Serial	115 Kbps	Mice/External modems
Parallel	500 Kbps	Printers/External Zip drives
USB 1.1	12 Mbps	Mice/Keyboards/Printers/Scanners/Game controllers
USB 2.0	400 Mbps	Same as USB 1.1 but at faster transfer rates. Also, camcorders, digital cameras, and MP3 players. It maintains compatibility with USB 1.1.
USB 3.0	5 Gbps	Same as USB 2.0 plus high-def video, music, and digital imaging applications. Backward compatible with USB 2.0.
FireWire/FireWire 800	400 Mbps/800 Mbps	Digital video camcorders/Digital cameras
Ethernet/Gigabit Ethernet	Up to 100 Mbps/Up to 1,000 Mbps	Network connections/Cable modems

Figure 62   Ports and their uses.

Figure 63   An Ethernet port and an Ethernet connector.

have made the older serial and parallel ports obsolete. Because of the USB port's speedy data transfer rate and its capability to be used with numerous devices, new computers often include six or more USB ports. Devices using USB ports include keyboards, mice, printers, scanners, digital cameras, MP3 players, and PDAs. In general, it's a good idea to get a computer with as many USB ports as possible. See the table in **Figure 62** for information about ports and their uses.

The *FireWire port,* developed by Apple and also known as IEEE 1394, is another means of transferring data quickly. The FireWire 400 has a data transfer rate of 400 Mbps, while the newer FireWire 800 transfers data at a blazing 800 Mbps! This port is typically used to connect devices that need to transfer huge amounts of data to a computer quickly, such as digital cameras, *digital video recorders,* or external hard drives. FireWire ports are standard on many Apple products, but are usually found only on higher-end Windows PCs and peripheral devices. Some peripheral devices offer users a choice of connecting using a USB port or a FireWire port.

What kind of port is used to connect to another computer? Connectivity ports, such as Ethernet and modem ports, are used to connect a computer to a local network or to the Internet. An *Ethernet port,* also known as an RJ-45 jack, resembles a standard phone jack, but is slightly larger as shown in **Figure 63**.

■ **Continue to the next page to complete the objective.**

The Gigabit Ethernet port is used for network access and can also be used to connect a cable modem or router for Internet access as shown in **Figure 64**. A *phone port* is the same size and shape as a phone jack, shown in **Figure 65**, and is then used to connect the modem to a phone system, enabling *digital subscriber line (DSL)* or dial-up Internet access as shown in Figure 64. DSL is a type of communications line in which signals travel through copper wires between a telephone switching station and a home or business as shown in **Figure 65**. The maximum data transfer rate for a modem is 56 Kbps, whereas the most common Ethernet standard, Fast Ethernet, transfers data at the rate of 100 Mbps. However, Gigabit Ethernet, with a potential transfer rate of 1,000 Mbps, is becoming an option on higher-end systems and is standard on many Mac systems.

Even faster Ethernet technologies, such as 10 Gigabit Ethernet or 10 GbE exist, are currently used for network backbones and enterprise network infrastructures rather than home users.

Are there special purpose ports? Despite the prevalence of USB ports, there are still some devices that require special ports. These ports include IrDA, Bluetooth, video, and audio ports.

MIDI ports, used to be used to connect electronic musical devices, such as keyboards and synthesizers, to a computer, enabling musicians to create digital music files. However, these ports have since been replaced by USB ports which are usually plug-and-play and don't require any software configuration.

■ **Continue to the next page to complete the objective.**

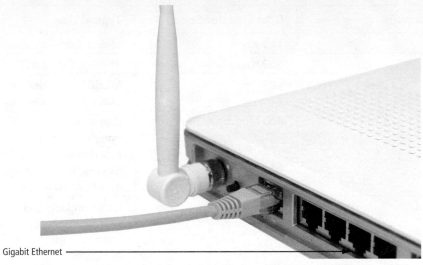

Gigabit Ethernet ——————————

Figure 64   Gigabit Ethernet ports allow for connecting a modem or router to the Internet.

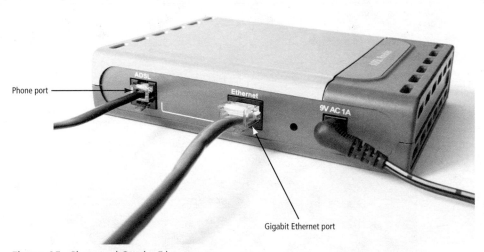

Phone port ———————

Gigabit Ethernet port

Figure 65   Phone and Gigabit Ethernet ports.

Bluetooth headset

Figure 66 Many wireless keyboards, PDAs, and other devices use a radio technology called Bluetooth to communicate over short devices.

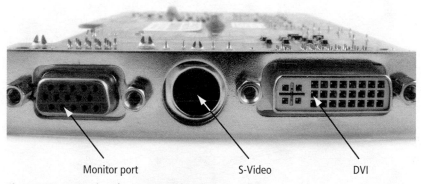

Monitor port   S-Video   DVI

Figure 67 Examples of monitor, S-Video, and DVI parts.

The ***IrDA port*** is used to enable devices such as PDAs, keyboards, mice, and printers to transmit data wirelessly to another device by using infrared light waves. In order to transmit information, each of the devices must have an IrDA port and a clear line of sight, with no other objects blocking the transmission.

Bluetooth is another type of wireless technology that relies on radio wave transmission and doesn't require a clear line of sight. Bluetooth-enabled devices such as smartphones, as shown in **Figure 66**, or other mobile devices can communicate only with each other over short distances, typically less than 30 feet.

Video ports include standard monitor ports, DVI ports, and S-video ports as shown in **Figure 67**. A ***monitor port*** is used to connect the monitor to the graphics processing unit, which is usually located on the motherboard or on a video card. However, to get the best results from a flat-panel (LCD) monitor, the ***Digital Video Interface (DVI) port*** should be used instead. The DVI port transmits a pure digital signal, eliminating the need for digital-to-analog conversion and resulting in a higher quality transmission and a clearer picture on the monitor. The ***S-video port*** is typically used to connect other video sources, such as a television, projector, or digital recorder, to the computer.

■ **Continue to the next page to complete the objective.**

Similar to video ports, *audio ports* connect audio devices, such as speakers, headphones, and *microphone*s, as shown in **Figure 68**, to the computer's sound card. These jacks will be familiar to anyone who is used to using standard stereo components.

Evaluating Your System

Each computer might have a different configuration. The way a computer system is set up or the combination of components that make up the system is called its *configuration*. This is important when buying a computer, expanding an existing system, or when connecting computers together in a network environment as shown in **Figure 69**.

Now that you have learned most of the hardware components of a typical personal computer, you are ready to explore the computer's configuration, specifications, and features. If you didn't buy your computer brand new, you might not know all the details about your computer. If you did buy a new computer, the easiest way is to check your paperwork; all the basic information should be there. However, if your computer isn't new or you didn't keep the paperwork, there are some ways to determine exactly what is in your system. Also if you start a new job or a new position and are given a computer system, you can do a number of things again to determine exactly what is in your system.

■ **Continue to the next page to complete the objective.**

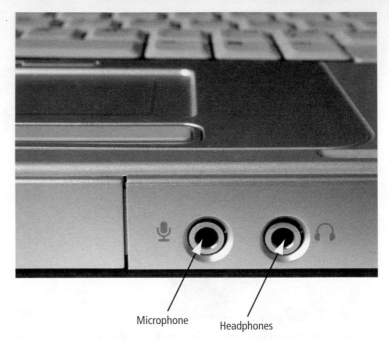

Microphone   Headphones

Figure 68   Audio ports are used to connect microphones and headphones to a computer.

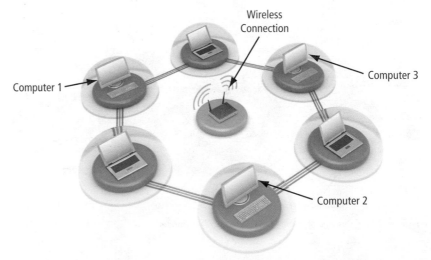

Figure 69   The networking configuration and the way the computer is set up allows sharing of resources.

Windows 7 users

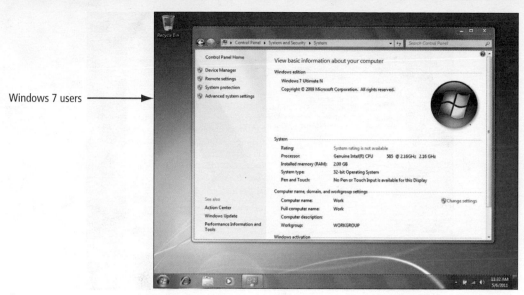

Figure 70   System Properties–Windows 7 users.

Windows Vista users

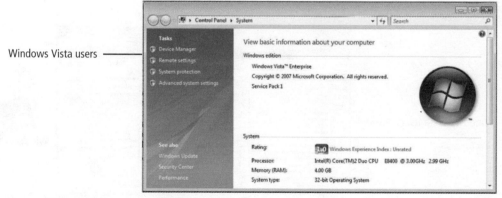

Figure 71   System Properties–Windows Vista users.

What kind of computer do you have? This is one of the easiest questions to answer. Like almost every other appliance you've used, you can probably find the manufacturer's name and a brand name or model number on the case of the computer. If not, check the back of the unit; there should be a metal tag that includes the manufacturer's name, model number, and serial number. This information might be necessary if you have to have service performed under warranty. Use the following steps to see your system properties on the screen, which will answer some questions.

If you are a Windows 7 user, follow these steps:

1. Click the **Start** menu, select **Control Panel,** and then click **System and Security.**

2. From the next window, click **System**. See **Figure 70**.

Windows Vista users can follow these steps:

1. Right-click the **My Computer** icon on the desktop and select **Properties**.

2. If the icon is not on the desktop, open the **Start** menu and then right-click the **Computer** button and select **Properties**. See **Figure 71**.

■ **Continue to the next page to complete the objective.**

What operating system does the computer use? If you watch carefully as a computer boots up, you can often determine the operating system. You will usually see a *splash screen* showing the version of Windows that runs—for example, Windows 7, Windows ME, Windows XP, or Windows Vista.

How do you determine what drives are on the system and how much storage space is available? It's important to know how much information you can store on your computer, what disk drives are available, and how much room you have left on each drive. **Figures 72** and **73** display windows with information on which drives are available. Is there enough storage space or are the storage devices getting full? Use My Computer (or Computer) to find the answers. If the desktop does not have a My Computer (or Computer) icon, you can access it through the Start menu.

■ **Continue to the next page to complete the objective.**

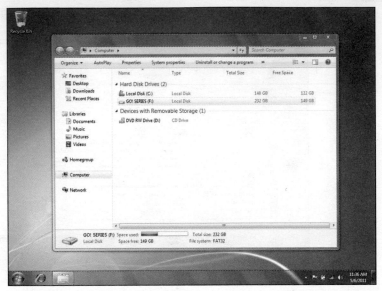

Figure 72   Using Windows Explorer to view the drives available to your computer—Windows 7 users.

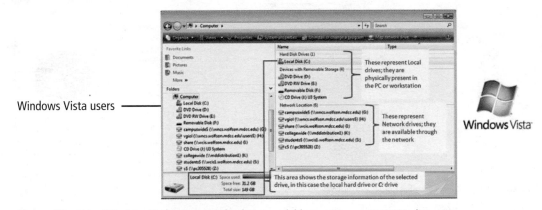

Windows Vista users

Figure 73   Using Windows Explorer to view the drives available to your computer—Windows Vista.

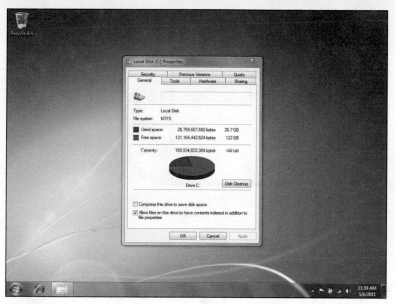

Figure 74   The properties of one of the storage drives (the hard drive).

The Computer (or Windows Explorer) window displays all available local drives (devices within the system unit or peripherals to that unit) and network drives (devices available through a network). Right-click on any drive symbol, and select Properties from the shortcut menu to display the drive's information similar to the one shown in **Figure 74**. The pie chart displayed on the General tab is a good visual tool that shows the size of your storage device and how much space is free.

Done! You have completed OBJECTIVE 3 of 6.

► Without software, the computer would just be a collection of useless electronic and mechanical parts.

► There are two categories of computer software—*system software* and *application software*. Both types of software are required to work effectively with your computer.

Software provides the instructions or commands that tell the computer what to do. To perform various tasks, the computer requires a set of instructions called *programs*. These programs enable individuals to use the computer without the need for special programming skills. **Figure 75** displays an example of software provided via a disk that users would then purchase and download onto their computer.

System Software

System software provides the instructions that the computer needs to run. It contains the directions needed to interface or interact with the computer and its peripheral devices so that you can use them. System software consists of two main programs: the *operating system* and *utility programs*, as shown in **Figure 76**.

■ **Continue to the next page to complete the objective.**

Figure 75 Software suites provide users with a cheaper method of obtaining all the software they want in one bundle.

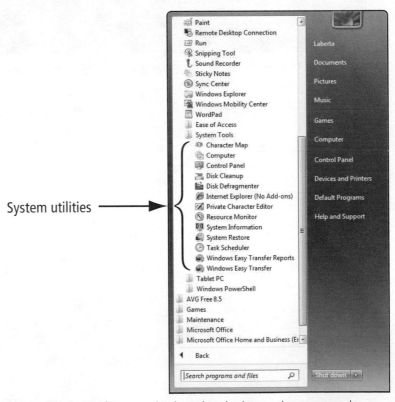

System utilities ⟶

Figure 76 Some utilities run only when selected; others can be programmed to run on a regular schedule.

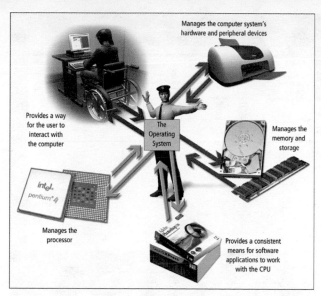

Figure 77 The operating system.

Operating Systems

What is the operating system? The **operating system (OS)** is a computer program that is present on every desktop computer, notebook, smartphone, or mainframe. The operating system controls how the computer works. As shown in **Figure 77**, the operating system manages the hardware components, including the CPU, memory, storage devices, peripheral devices, and network devices. It also coordinates with the various software applications presently running and provides the interaction with the user.

Is it possible to communicate with the operating system? Although the operating system communicates with the computer and its peripherals, it also includes a **user interface** that you can use to interact and communicate with the computer. Early operating systems used a text-based or keyboard-driven interface. The early **Disk Operating System (DOS)** required knowledge of special commands that had to be typed to achieve the desired results. This type of system was not very **user friendly.** Most current operating systems use a point-and-click format known as a **graphical user interface (GUI).** GUIs are more user friendly and intuitive than DOS systems.

Rather than typing specific commands, you can use a mouse to select screen objects such as **icons** (a graphical depiction of an object such as a file or program) as shown in **Figure 78**, *menus*

■ **Continue to the next page to complete the objective.**

Icons

Figure 78 Icons are used to open a file, window or program, for example.

(lists of available commands), or *dialog boxes* (windows used to make choices or give the system specific instructions as to the action you want to take or task to perform). GUI operating systems display information on the monitor in the form of rectangular boxes called *windows* as shown in **Figure 79**. Although you interact with system software every time you use the computer, in some ways you don't notice it.

Do all computers need an operating system? Yes, the operating system is a critical part of a computer system. Without an OS to provide specific instructions, the computer would be unable to fulfill its four main functions. However, different computers require different types of operating systems. There are several popular operating systems available for home computers. They include Microsoft Windows, Mac OS, and Linux.

Microsoft Windows has the largest market share of the three main operating systems and is found on most of today's desktop and notebook computers. There have been many versions of Microsoft Windows, including Windows 3.0, Windows 95, Windows 98, Windows ME, Windows Vista, and Windows 7. Although a previous version of Windows might be found on an older computer, Windows 7 is the current version installed on most new computers. A sample Windows 7 desktop is displayed in **Figure 80**.

■ Continue to the next page to complete the objective. ➤

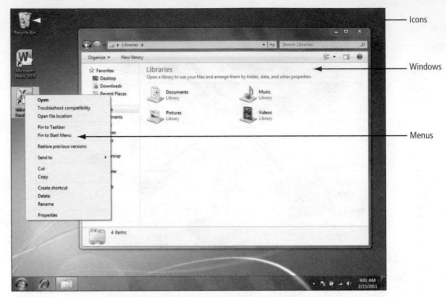

Figure 79 Windows are rectangular boxes that display information on the computer.

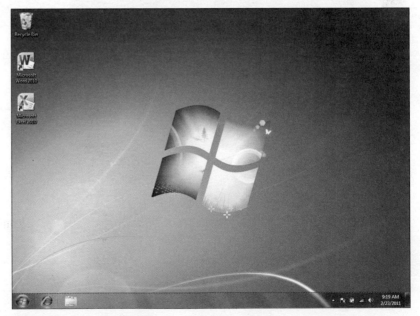

Figure 80 A sample of the Windows 7 desktop.

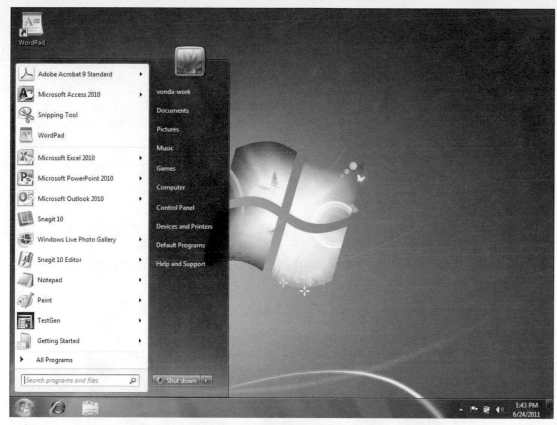

Figure 81 Windows operating system with Microsoft Office installed.

Why are there so many versions of Windows? Software developers are always updating and refining their software to adapt to new technology, respond to vulnerabilities, and improve their product. Because Microsoft also manufactures application software, some of its products have similar names and users can become confused. It's important to note that even though your computer might use Microsoft Windows for its operating system, as shown in **Figure 81**, it might not have Microsoft Office (an application software suite) installed.

The *Mac OS* is an operating system designed specifically for Apple's Macintosh computers.

The Mac OS desktop is similar to Windows because it also uses a GUI. In fact, Apple was the first company to introduce a commercially successful GUI operating system for the consumer market. But, because of the popularity of the Windows-based PCs, Mac OS has a much smaller market share. If you are looking to purchase a PC or a peripheral for a PC, you have a variety of choices among different manufacturers. Only Apple manufactures Apple products and peripherals for its computers, and they tend to be a bit pricier.

Can Windows run on an Apple computer? Until recently, the Windows OS could not run on a Mac. Software is available to start a Mac that will run Windows applications. **Figure 82** demonstrates the features in Microsoft's Virtual PC for Mac. In addition, Mac offers a built-in utility on certain Mac operating systems called Boot Camp which allows users to run Windows XP, Windows Vista, Windows 7 or Linux operating systems on a Mac computer.

- Access PC software, files, networks, and devices with your Mac
- Zero-configuration printing; better graphics handling; expanded preferences
- Cut and paste between platforms; share folders and other media between platforms
- Easily shut down virtual PC and relaunch right where it left off
- Use PC and Mac peripherals

Figure 82 Microsoft's virtual PC for Mac features specifications such as:

■ **Continue to the next page to complete the objective.**

Linux is an alternative operating system. Based on the UNIX operating system developed for mainframe computers, it also has a dedicated group of users. Linux is an ***open-source*** operating system, which means it is not owned by a single company and some versions are available at no cost. See the table in **Figure 83**.

How is open-source software different from other types of software? Open-source software makes its source code, essentially the program instructions, available to anyone who would like to see it. Programmers are encouraged to work with and change the code as they see fit, in the hope that having many "eyes" looking at the code will streamline and improve it. Proprietary software, such as Microsoft Windows, keeps this code secret and inaccessible to programmers who are not authorized by the software development company.

Why is Linux used? Linux is rarely used by novice computer users, although it is popular among developers and other technologically advanced individuals who prefer to use an alternative operating system as shown in **Figure 84**. Some people appreciate the opportunity to work in this more "open" programming

■ **Continue to the next page to complete the objective.**

Software Type	Example	Description
Open source software	Linux OpenOffice.org suite Google Docs	Non-proprietary software that is sometimes available at no cost
Proprietary software	Microsoft Windows and Office Apple Mac OS X iWork	Proprietary software available to users at a cost

Figure 83 Examples of open source software and proprietary software.

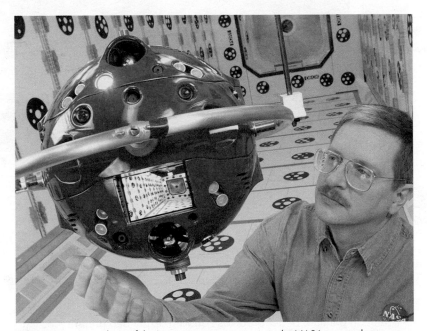

Figure 84 A novel use of the Linux operating system is in the NASA personal satellite assistant, currently under development. The six-inch sphere will float around the International Space Station and act as an environmental monitor and communications device. Its design was inspired by the light saber training droid used by Luke Skywalker in the movie *Star Wars*.

Figure 85 Example of one of the versions of the Linux operating system.

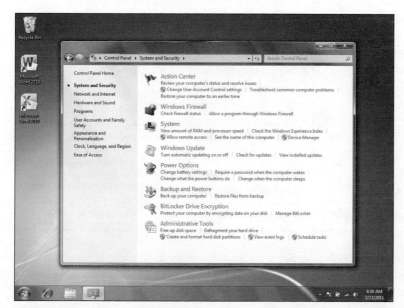

Figure 86 Utility programs in Windows 7.

environment. However, one of the disadvantages of Linux is that, because no single company is responsible for it, technical support is not easily found. Users might find help from various resources such as user groups and Internet communities. Alternatively, some software companies have chosen to develop and sell a version of Linux that includes a warranty and technical support as a way of alleviating user concerns. **Figure 85** shows an example of one version of the Linux operating system.

Utility Programs

What are utility programs? Operating system software is the most critical software on the computer, because nothing can run without it. However, *utility programs,* as shown in **Figure 86**, are another important component of system software. These small applications handle many important tasks involved with the management and maintenance of your system. Utility programs can be used to help back up important files, remove unwanted files or programs from your system, and schedule various tasks to keep your system running smoothly. Some of these utilities are included with the operating system, whereas others are standalone versions that you can purchase or download for free.

■ **Continue to the next page to complete the objective.**

The table in **Figure 87** displays various utility programs that are provided with the Windows operating system and compares them with similar stand-alone products, describing the function of each utility.

Application Software

Application software is comprised of programs that enable you to accomplish tasks and use the computer in a productive manner. Applications are programs created to perform a specific task or address a specific need.

How do system software and application software work together? System software is like breathing; you usually don't think about it unless something goes wrong. Application software can be compared to an instrument like a flute. When a musician combines each of these breaths with the flute, the result may be a beautiful melody. Computer software works similarly; the system software acts as the "breath," while the application software provides the "instrument," enabling you to create something.

There are many different kinds of application software, although they often fall into one of several categories including financial and business-related software, graphics and multimedia software, educational and reference software, entertainment software, and communication software. You might be most familiar with productivity software, which includes the following applications.

Word processing software is used to create, edit, format, print, and save documents

■ **Continue to the next page to complete the objective.**

Program	Function
• Windows Explorer	Create folders, manage files, and compress/extract files. Read disk drive's properties including view storage capacity and free disk space, check drive for errors, defragment utility, and back up/restore utility
• Windows Task Manager	Lets the user view the list of active applications and switch or end any of them. Also, check the performance of the computer including CPU usage, RAM availability, and network utilization
Control Panel • System and Security	Review your computer's status Back up your computer Find and fix problems
• Network and Internet	View network status and tasks Choose home group and sharing options
• Hardware and sound	View devices and printers Add a device Connect to a projector Adjust commonly used mobility settings
• Programs	Install/uninstall programs Add desktop gadgets
• User Accounts and Family Safety	Add or remove user accounts Set up parental controls for any user
• Appearance and Personalization	Change the theme Change desktop background Adjust screen resolution Change keyboards or other input methods
• Clock, Language, and Region	Change display language Let Windows suggest settings
• Ease of Access	Optimizes visual display
Administrative Tools	**Function**
Security • Security Configuration Manager • Firewall and Advanced Security	Set account policies, local policies, network list manager policies, software restriction policies, and application control policies Set firewall and advanced security on local computer

Figure 87 Windows utility programs.

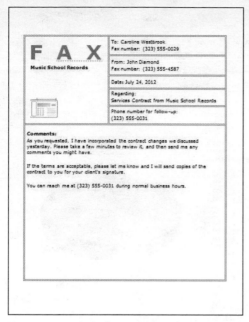

Figure 88 Sample document created with Microsoft Word 2010.

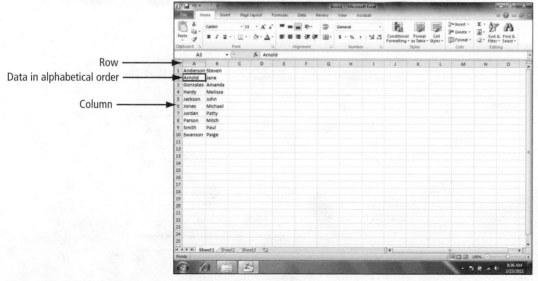

Figure 89 Microsoft Excel is an example of spreadsheet software.

and other text-based files. Word processing software enables you to create or edit letters, reports, memos, and many other types of written documents that you can print or attach to an email message. Revisions to existing documents can be made quickly and easily, without having to re-create the entire document. Documents created with this type of software can also include pictures, charts, hyperlinks, and other graphic elements. A *hyperlink* is a connection to another area of a document or a connection to an Internet URL. Microsoft Word, Lotus Word Pro, and Corel WordPerfect are all examples of word processing programs. A document created using Microsoft Word 2010 is shown in **Figure 88**. Notice that the document contains a graphic element as well as text.

Using word processing software replaces the use of conventional typewriters, on which editing was virtually impossible once the document was finished.

Spreadsheet software, as shown in **Figure 89**, enables the user to enter data in rows and columns format and:

- Perform calculations on numeric data with user-defined formulas.

- Convert part of the data into one or more charts, such as a column chart, a pie chart, or a line chart.

- Work with lists to organize data and sort it in alphabetic or numeric order.

- Create different scenarios and perform "what-if" analyses, the basis for sound decision making.

■ **Continue to the next page to complete the objective.**

A key advantage of spreadsheet software is its capability to recalculate values without user intervention. When data used in a calculation or a formula is changed, the spreadsheet software automatically updates the worksheet with the correct result. Microsoft Excel, Lotus 1-2-3, and Corel Quattro Pro are examples of spreadsheet programs. **Figure 90** shows a worksheet and a chart created with Microsoft Excel 2010. The use of spreadsheet software replaces the old manual method of entering data in ledgers or journals and using a desktop calculator to do the math computations.

A ***database*** is a collection of data or unorganized facts. ***Database software*** is used to store, organize, update, and retrieve large amounts of data making websites, as shown in **Figure 91**, possible. ***Relational database software (RDBMS)*** stores information in tables, which enable users' quick access to the data by connecting tables with common fields. ***Data mining*** is a function in some databases that looks for hidden patterns in the data to anticipate future patterns. This is commonly used in scientific applications and as a marketing tool to predict future consumer trends. Typically, database software can be used to manage various types of information, such as that found in large mailing lists, inventories, students' records, order histories, and invoicing. Databases help you to enter, store, sort, filter, retrieve, and summarize the information they contain and then generate meaningful

■ **Continue to the next page to complete the objective.**

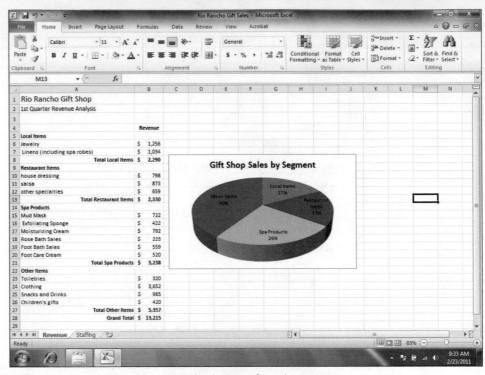

Figure 90 Example spreadsheet created with Microsoft Excel 2010.

Figure 91 Internet auction websites, such as Amazon.com, wouldn't be possible without database technology.

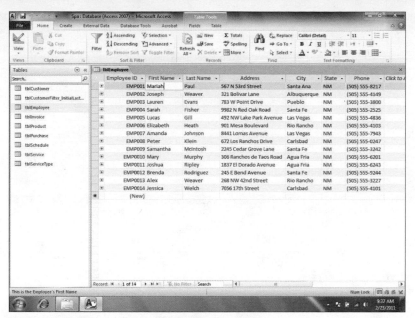

Figure 92 Examples of database software objects.

Figure 93 Example presentation created with Microsoft PowerPoint 2010.

reports. Common database programs include Microsoft Access, Lotus Approach, and Corel Paradox. **Figure 92** shows a database object created in Microsoft Access 2010. Database software replaces an old manual filing system where information is stored in filing cabinets in a single location.

Presentation software has replaced flip charts, slide projectors, and overhead transparencies used by speakers and lecturers. This software is used to create electronic slides and project slide shows to visually present materials and ideas to large groups in a conference room or on the Web. Presentation software is also used to create audience handouts, speaker notes, and other materials that can be used during an oral presentation or for distribution to a group of participants. Microsoft PowerPoint, Lotus Freelance Graphics, and Corel Presentations are examples of presentation software programs. **Figure 93** shows a presentation created with Microsoft PowerPoint 2010.

Communication and organizational software—Communication software can cover a broad range of tasks including videoconferencing and telephony. However, applications in the productivity category are most often used to send and receive email. These applications typically include an address book (contacts list), a scheduler, a calendar, and task functions help users organize their personal and

■ **Continue to the next page to complete the objective.**

professional responsibilities. Microsoft Outlook, Lotus Notes, and Corel WordPerfect Mail are examples of communication and organizational software. **Figure 94** shows an example of a calendar in Microsoft Outlook 2010.

What is a software suite? Although it is possible to buy any of the previous applications separately, most software manufacturers, including Microsoft, Corel, and Lotus, also group applications together into a package called a ***suite***. There are also alternative suites such as Google Docs and OpenOffice, which are free. They are designed as an open source software in such a way that users can report bugs, request new features, or change and improve the software.

Another advantage of using a suite is that products from the same company have many common elements, such as basic window design and layout, toolbars containing similar tools, dictionaries, and media galleries, so many users find this familiarity makes it easier to switch between the programs in a suite. Examples of suites include Microsoft Office, Corel WordPerfect Office, and Lotus SmartSuite.

What are some other common software applications? Recall that there are many different types of application software besides productivity software, each one with a specific function as shown in the table in **Figure 95**. Some of these are the following:

- You might use Microsoft Publisher or QuarkXPress to create newsletters or brochures.

■ **Continue to the next page to complete the objective.**

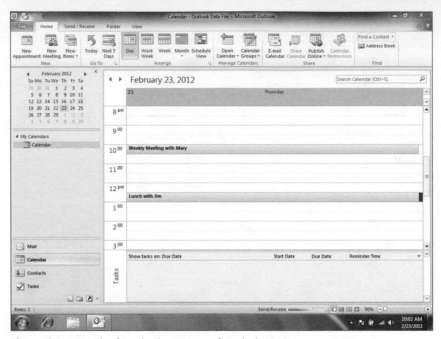

Figure 94 Example of a calendar in Microsoft Outlook 2010.

Category	Program	Manufacturer
Desktop publishing	Publisher QuarkXPress	Microsoft Quark
Paint/image editor	Painter Paint	Corel Microsoft
Drawing/design	Illustrator AutoCAD CorelDraw Graphics Visio	Adobe Autodesk Corel Microsoft
Photo/image editing	PhotoShop PhotoShop Elements PaintShop Photo Pro Picassa GIMP	Adobe Adobe Corel Google

Figure 95 Common drawing, image editing and photo editing applications.

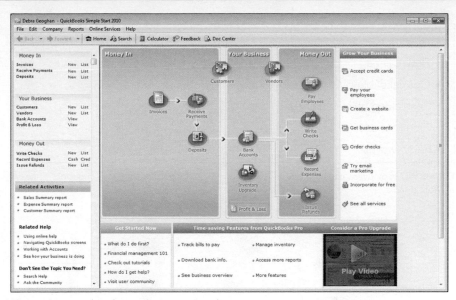

Figure 96 QuickBooks Simple Start 2010 edition.

Figure 97 Mint.com is an online financial management tool.

- Bookkeepers rely on special accounting packages such as Peachtree Accounting or QuickBooks to balance the books and handle other accounting functions. See **Figure 96**.

- Graphic designers turn to packages such as Adobe Photoshop or Adobe Illustrator to develop creative artwork.

- You might use Microsoft Expression Web or Macromedia Dreamweaver to create your own website.

- *IM (instant messaging)* software enables users to communicate in real time like a phone conversation but using text only. The software can alert you if a member of your group is online at that moment.

- Web browsers are software used to locate and display web pages and navigate through them. They also enable users to store their frequently used sites for quick access.

If you have a specific need, chances are there is software that will address those needs such as the online financial management tool shown in **Figure 97**. Today the best way to find software is to do a web search using a search engine.

Done! You have completed Objective 4 of 6.

▶ Connecting one computer to another creates a *network*.

▶ Some of the benefits of computer networks include the capability to share data, software, and resources such as printers, scanners, Internet access, video conferencing, and VoIP.

What are the components of a network? Recall that computers and the various peripherals that are connected to them are called hardware. Networks consist of two or more connected computers, which can be connected using several media as shown in **Figure 98**, plus the various peripheral devices that are attached to them. Each object connected to a network, whether it is a computer or a peripheral device, is known as a *node*.

Wireless networks use radio waves instead of wires or cables to connect. Most networks use a combination of media and wireless communications as shown in **Figure 99**.

Today, using computer networks, institutions are able to *video conference,* that is, communicate audio and/or video between two or more individuals in different locations, optimizing communications, information sharing, and decision making.

Voice over Internet Protocol (VoIP) enables voice, facsimile, and voice-messaging communications over networks and the Internet.

■ **Continue to the next page to complete the objective.**

- Existing telephone wires
- Power lines
- Coaxial cables
- Unshielded twisted pair (UTP) cables
- Fiber optic
- Radio waves

Figure 98 Computers can be connected to a network using several media, the conductors of the network signals.

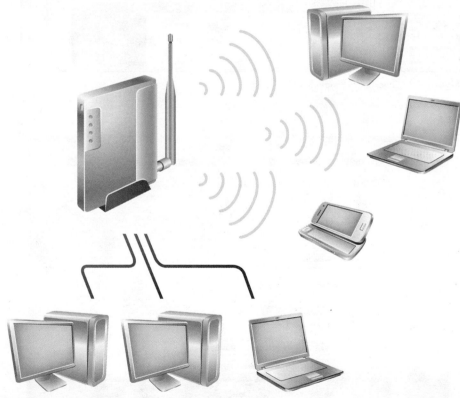

Figure 99 A network using both wireless and wires.

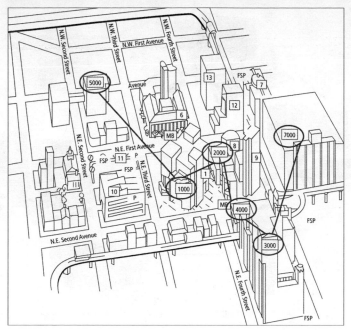

Figure 100 Example of a local area network, a college campus network that covers several buildings within a few city blocks.

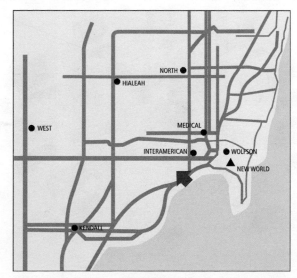

Figure 101 Example of a wide area network, which is a college network that links campus LANs in several cities within a county.

Can networks be different sizes? A network that connects computers reasonably close together, say within a few city blocks in adjacent buildings, is called a ***local area network (LAN).*** See **Figure 100**.

If the network grows to cover a larger geographic area or includes other networks, it becomes a ***wide area network (WAN).*** An example is a college campus that connects its computers with a LAN while all of its campuses connected together form a WAN, as shown in **Figure 101**. Because the different campuses are connected through WANs, students, faculty, and staff can easily use the resources of the entire network. Both LANs and WANs can be wired, wireless, or a combination of both. The Internet is the largest WAN as it connects computer networks all around the world.

Are networks public or private? They can be either. If you want to post information and make it available to any user, you post it on a website with no restrictions. If you want to protect certain information, you create an ***intranet*** in which access is restricted to authorized users only. Within an intranet, network administrators can limit the specific rights and privileges of different users.

How are networks configured? Networks can be configured in several ways. There are two main categories: peer-to-peer and client/server. ***Peer-to-peer*** or ***P2P networks*** are most commonly found in homes and small businesses. In a peer-to-peer network, each node can communicate with every other node without a dedicated server or hierarchy among computers. Peer-to-peer networks are relatively

■ **Continue to the next page to complete the objective.**

easy to set up, but tend to be small as shown in **Figure 102**. This makes them ideal for home use, although not as desirable in the workplace. If a network grows to more than, say, ten to fifteen nodes, it is generally best to use the *client/server network*. In a client/server network, the server manages and controls all network resources. A *node* can be a computer, printer, scanner, modem, an external hard disk, or any other peripheral device connected to a computer. Therefore, it isn't difficult to find ten or more nodes in an office or business setting.

How is a client/server network different from a P2P network? Client/server networks typically have two different types of computers as shown in **Figure 103**. The *client* is the computer used at your desk or workstation to write letters, send email, produce invoices, or perform any of the many tasks that can be accomplished with a computer. The client computer is the one most people directly interact with. In contrast, the *server* computer is typically kept in a secure location and is used by network technicians and administrators to manage network resources. If a server is assigned to handle only specific tasks, it is known as a *dedicated server.* For instance, a web server is used to store and deliver web pages, a file server is used to store and archive files, and a print server manages the printing resources for the network. Each of these is a dedicated server.

■ **Continue to the next page to complete the objective.**

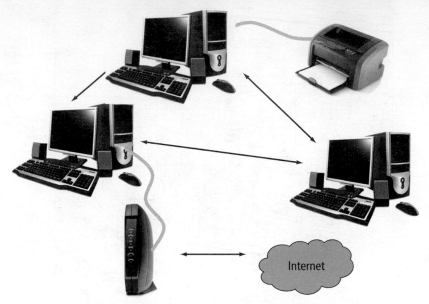

Figure 102   Peer-to-peer networks have no servers. Users share resources equally.

Figure 103   A client-server network with a centralized server.

As a client/server network grows in number of nodes and geographical distance, servers are assisted by distance-spanning devices such as switches and routers to optimize data traffic as shown in **Figure 104**.

Done! You have completed Objective 5 of 6.

Figure 104 Six ethernet switches.

► Being computer competent implies you are a responsible computer user. This means more than just understanding the key components of a computer or the differences between hardware and software.

► Responsible computer users also know how to properly maintain their computers, back up necessary data, and protect themselves and others from security breaches and attacks.

Computer Maintenance

The first step to protect your computer and the valuable information it contains is to establish a regular maintenance routine. **Figure 105** shows an example of an antivirus software program that can help to protect your software. In addition, backup utility programs, which may be part of your system software or purchased separately, enable you to back up your files as shown in **Figure 106**. You can back up everything on your computer, just one or two important files, or anything in between. People often think that the computer is the most expensive item to replace if their hard drive fails. In reality, it is usually all the lost information that was contained on the hard drive that is the most costly to replace, if it is even possible to do so. Think about the types of files you might have on your own computer like financial records, your personal phone/address

■ **Continue to the next page to complete the objective.**

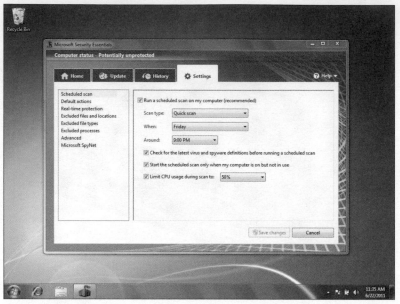

Figure 105 Antivirus software, such as Microsoft Security Essentials, provides for automatic updates to the software installed on the computer.

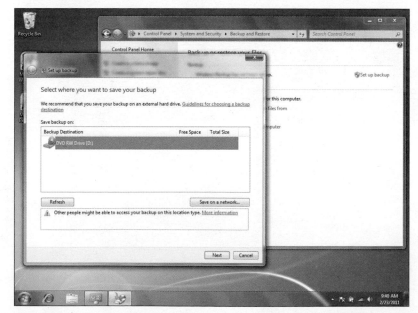

Figure 106 A backup utility program available through Microsoft Windows 7.

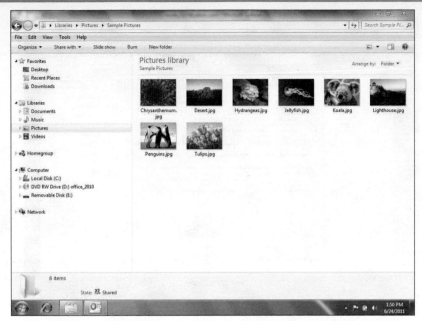

Figure 107 Personal files such as your photos can be lost forever if you fail to back them up.

Figure 108 Several utilities are available through the Systems folder which allow you to perform regular file maintenance.

directory, resumes, scanned images of important documents, homework or school projects, your CD collection and purchased music files, and family photos and videos. See **Figure 107**. Now imagine how you would re-create these files if they were irretrievably damaged. Would you be able to find them again? If you back up files on a regular basis and store the backups in a secure location, you lessen the impact that a mechanical failure or security breach will have on your data.

What other types of maintenance tasks should be performed? In addition to backing up files, regular file maintenance also helps to maintain your system. Several useful Windows utilities can be accessed from the System Tools folder. You can access the System Tools folder by clicking Start, clicking All Programs, and then clicking Accessories as shown in **Figure 108**. Disk Cleanup scans the hard drive and removes unnecessary files such as those found in the Recycle Bin, in addition to temporary Internet files and other temporary files created by various programs. It is possible to adjust the settings and select which files to delete and which files to retain.

Similarly, the Disk Defragmenter scans the hard drive. However, rather than removing files, it attempts to reallocate files so they use the available hard drive space more efficiently. Recall that data is stored on hard drives in sectors and tracks.

■ **Continue to the next page to complete the objective.**

As file sizes change, they can outgrow their original location. When that happens, the remaining portion of the file may be stored elsewhere. If a file size decreases, or a file is deleted, this can create a blank area on the hard drive.

Defragmenting a hard drive enables scattered portions of files to be regrouped and open spaces to be rearranged. This results in faster and more efficient file access, which improves the response time of the hard drive.

Is there a way to automate these maintenance tasks? Running these programs can be time-consuming, especially when you want to use your computer for other tasks. It is also easy to forget to do these things on a regular basis. That is why newer versions of Windows include a Task Scheduler. This utility enables you to create a task and select the best time for each task to run, in addition to how often, which makes the whole process automatic. **Figures 109** and **110** show the Task Scheduler dialog box for Windows 7 users and Windows Vista users, respectively.

Can changes to my system be undone? Sometimes when new software is installed on a computer, the results are not what you anticipated. Instead of playing a new game, you find your system stops responding each time you start it. Or, you might find the new driver you installed for your printer is causing conflicts. Even though you've tried to uninstall the software, the system is still not right.

■ **Continue to the next page to complete the objective.**

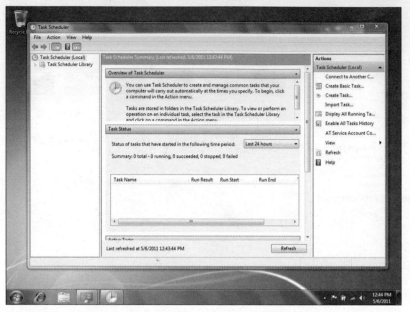

Figure 109 Computer maintenance—Task Scheduler (Windows 7 users).

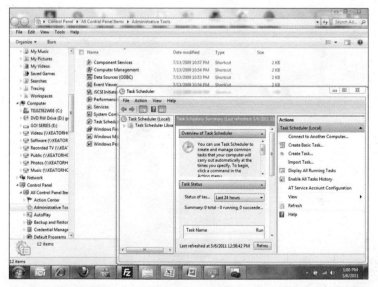

Figure 110 Computer maintenance—steps to set a task in the Task Scheduler (Windows Vista users).

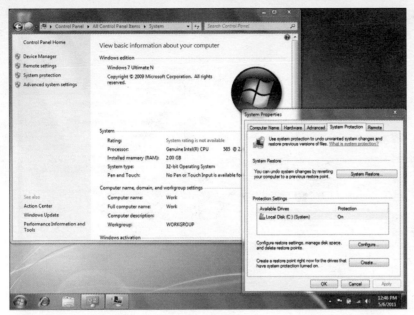

Figure 111 Windows 7 System Properties dialog box where the System Restore is accessible.

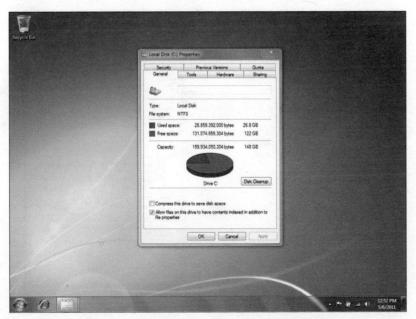

Figure 112 Computer maintenance—steps to access Disk Cleanup (Windows 7 users).

If you are running a newer version of Windows, the System Restore utility comes to the rescue. Periodically, Windows creates a *restore point*, which records all the settings for your system. It's similar to taking a picture of how everything is currently set up. **Figure 111** shows the System Properties dialog box for Windows 7 where the System Restore can be performed.

It is also possible to set manual restore points, and it is highly recommended that you do so before installing new software or hardware, or when making major changes to your system. If you experience a problem with your system after the new software is installed, you can roll your system back to an earlier restore point when the system was working correctly. Returning to an earlier restore point affects only your system settings. It does not delete any of the data files you may have created during the interval.

What other functions can you use to maintain a "healthy" computer? Following are some of the other things that keep computers healthy:

- *Disk Cleanup*—This is a group of tasks intended to free disk space cause by Internet temporary files and hard drive unwanted files that accumulate from time to time. Part of this routine includes emptying the Recycle Bin. **Figure 112** shows the steps for accessing Disk Cleanup in Windows 7.

■ **Continue to the next page to complete the objective.**

- **Activate and set up the Internet Pop-up Blocker**—This lets the user the select options to allow or to block advertising and other pop-up windows while surfing the Web. **Figures 113** show the steps for accessing Pop-up Blocker in Windows 7.

- **Access and set up Security settings**—You can set security settings, such as:
  - Check for security updates
  - Select the settings for the Windows Firewall
  - Check for Windows software updates
  - Scan for spyware and other potentially unwanted software
  - Change Internet security options

Figure 114 shows the steps for accessing security settings in Windows 7.

Establishing the habit of performing regular maintenance on your computer is one way to protect it, and yourself, from data loss. But there are many other dangers you need to be aware of too. Viruses, spyware, and *hackers* are all out there waiting to pounce on the unwary computer user. The term *hacker,* as used here, signifies an expert in computers and programming languages who uses his/her expertise to obtain unauthorized access to computer systems with the purpose corrupting data and/ or stealing information.

What are viruses and how do they get on the computer? Computer *viruses* are malicious codes or software designed to invade your computer system and obtain, alter, or destroy data without your knowledge and against your wishes.

■ **Continue to the next page to complete the objective.**

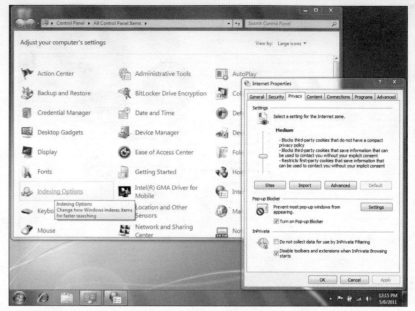

Figure 113   Computer maintenance—steps to access the Pop-up Blocker (Windows 7 users).

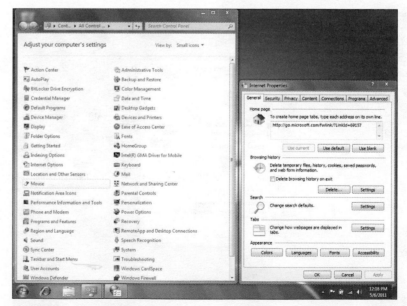

Figure 114   Computer maintenance—steps to access the security settings and other functions (Windows 7 users).

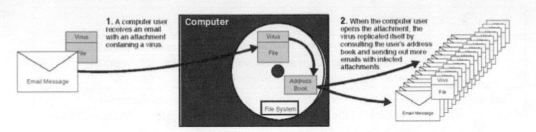

Figure 115 Only email attachments from trusted sources should be opened in order to reduce the possibility of receiving a virus.

Some viruses merely seem to be nuisances or might not even be obvious to the user; some cause files to be corrupted or erased; and others are capable of shutting down a computer and erasing the entire hard drive. Viruses infect a system and then attach themselves to a program or file to spread to other users.

Viruses can be distributed in several ways. In the early days of computers, viruses were spread by sharing infected floppy disks. Now, due to the ease in which files can be shared over the Internet, viruses are able to spread much more quickly. One of the most common ways to send a virus is through email attachments as shown in **Figure 115**. Security experts recommend you never open an email attachment unless you have first scanned it with antivirus software to determine that it is virus-free. Experts also recommend that unless you know the sender and have been expecting the email attachment, it is best to delete the attachment without ever opening it. There are also websites dedicated to providing information on common email scams as shown in **Figure 116**.

Are viruses and worms the same thing?
Worms are similar to viruses because they are also malicious programs that spread from computer to computer; however, unlike viruses, worms are able to do this without any human interaction and are able to replicate themselves so numerous copies can be sent. Worms can burrow into your email address book, or locate

■ **Continue to the next page to complete the objective.**

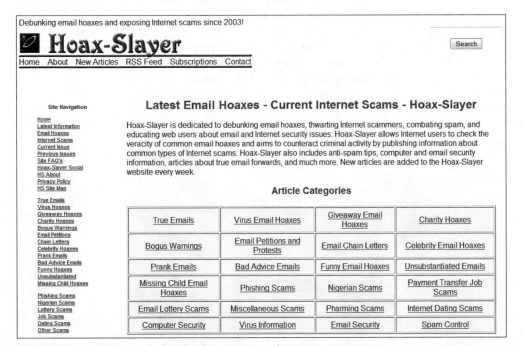

Figure 116 One place to check to see if a message is a hoax is Snopes.com.

email addresses on files saved on your hard drive, then send themselves out without any help from you. When it reaches the email recipient, it does the same thing to the recipient's address book. Also, because worms can quickly replicate themselves, they can repeat this scenario over and over. Just the sheer amount of traffic they cause on a network can be enough to bring an entire company to a grinding halt. Worms can also open a "back door" to your system, which enables hackers access to it and gives them the ability to control your computer remotely. See **Figure 117** for examples of worms that have been distributed in the past.

Trojan horses are not truly viruses because they do not duplicate themselves or infect other files; however, they can be just as problematic because they open your system for other intruders, such as *bots*, that may work together as a botnet, as shown in **Figure 118**. A *botnet* is a popular term for a group of software robots that run automatically in networks such as instant messengers, chat rooms, and discussion groups that have been made vulnerable by the presence of Trojan horses. Once inside a chat room, for instance, a botnet can generate *spam,* which is bulk unsolicited email messages to random lists of computer users. At first glance, a Trojan horse often appears to be a desirable software program, such as a free screensaver, but Trojan Horses facilitate unauthorized access to a computer system.

■ **Continue to the next page to complete the objective.**

Worm	Description
Sasser	Sasser is a worm that affects computers via network connections that are running vulnerable versions of the Microsoft operating systems Windows XP and Windows 2000.
Blaster	The Blaster worm attacked un-patched operating systems on computers running the Microsoft operating systems Windows XP and Windows 2000.
NetSky	The worm was sent out as an email. After recipients opened the attachment, the program would search the computer for email addresses and then spread by emailing itself to all of the addresses found on the recipients system.
MyDoom	MyDoom worm was also sent via email with an attachment and subject line that caused the recipient to believe there has been a transmission error such as "Error", "Mail Delivery System" or "Mail Transaction Failed". Once opened, the attachment would resend itself to addresses found on the recipients system, however avoided email addresses at Rutgers, MIT, Stanford, and UC Berkeley as well as the companies Microsoft and Symantec.

Figure 117 Worms that have created trouble in the past.

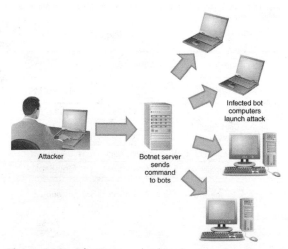

Figure 118 A botnet is used to launch an attack.

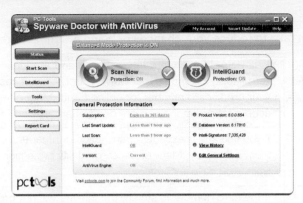

Figure 119 After performing a routine scan of a computer, Spyware Doctor will return a log of problems found on the system.

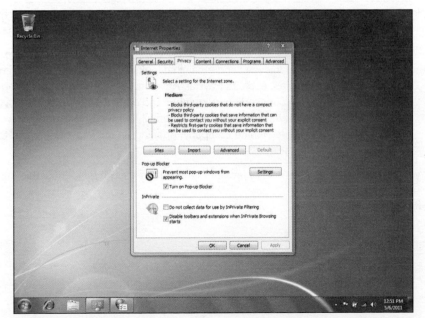

Figure 120 Tools are available through your browser (Internet Explorer is shown here) or as separate applications to distinguish between cookies you want to keep and cookies you don't want on your system.

Trojans come with an unwanted and hidden agenda. After the software is installed, the effects can be similar to those that viruses or worms cause. Before you install new software, it is important to scan the program files with antivirus software to ensure there are no Trojan horses lurking there. And, as with unknown email attachments, it is important to be skeptical about free software; it's not often that you really get something for nothing!

Spyware

How is spyware different from viruses?
Spyware is software designed to capture personal and confidential information that resides on your system and send it elsewhere. It has quickly become as large a problem as viruses. Spyware's primary threat is to your privacy and confidentiality. Although spyware is not usually intended to harm your system, it can sometimes have that effect on it. **Adware** is spyware that tracks your Internet browsing and can install cookies on your computer as shown. **Figure 119** is a spyware software program that can search for adware on your computer and provide a readout of where it is located.

A **cookie** is a small text file that contains information that can identify you to a website. Cookies are not necessarily bad. They are useful when they are used to help personalize your web browsing experience, but cookies can threaten your privacy if they are used to reveal too much information. Cookies can be filtered, eliminating cookies you don't want on your system as shown in **Figure 120**.

■ **Continue to the next page to complete the objective.**

How can you tell if malware is on a computer? One symptom is an increase in the number of pop-up ads the user receives, some of which might even address the user by name! Adware can generate pop-up ads even when you're not online. Some types of adware can also reset a web browser's home page to a page of its choosing and take control of the search engine, directing you to websites that have been predetermined by the adware.

Are there other privacy threats? Key loggers are another type of spyware. In this case, a software program records every keystroke you type. Key loggers can capture all sorts of confidential information this way—passwords, credit card numbers, bank account numbers, and so on—and then relay this information elsewhere. Entire email messages and instant messaging conversations can be recorded this way too. Some key loggers are hardware, rather than software, although they perform the same devious function. Such hardware devices can be attached between the keyboard and the computer. The information stolen through the use of key loggers can easily make you a victim of identity theft. Trojan horses can be used to distribute key loggers and other types of spyware just as easily as they deliver viruses.

How can you avoid being a victim? To minimize the risk of having malware installed on your computer, or from being a victim of identity theft in general, there are some practical precautions you can take, as shown in **Figure 121**. One of the most prevalent

■ **Continue to the next page to complete the objective.**

Precautions you can take to reduce your chances of being a victim of identity theft:	
Make all your online purchases using PayPal or a credit card.	Visa USA, MasterCard International, and American Express all have zero-liability programs that waive your liability in case someone uses your credit card number for online fraud. Most debit cards, checking accounts, and money orders don't offer this kind of protection.
Scan your bills and statements promptly.	If you find any unexpected transaction or other unpleasant surprises, report them right away. Many credit card liability protection programs have time limits—60 days is common.
Get a separate credit card with a low credit limit for your online transactions.	If the card number is stolen, the thieves will not be able to run up as large a balance.
Make sure a secure website is managing your online transaction.	Look at the address of the website you are visiting. The URL should begin with https, not http. The https designator means the site is using encryption to improve the security of the transaction.
Don't disclose personal information over the phone.	Remember that a credit card company would never call you and ask you for your credit card number, expiration date, or other personal information; they already know it.
Handle email with care.	Cunning thieves send email that looks like it comes from legitimate companies, such as PayPal, Amazon.com, or your bank asking you to update your credit card number and other personal information. But when you click the link in this kind of email, the website that loads isn't really from the legitimate company, opening up unsuspecting users to credit card theft.
Don't put your Social Security number or your driver's license number on your checks.	These are key pieces of information sought by identity thieves.

Figure 121 Protecting yourself from identity theft. (Source: Taken from *Digital Planet: Tomorrow's Technology and You*, 10e.)

Figure 122 Be cautious of emails sent to you as they can contain viruses and other harmful malware.

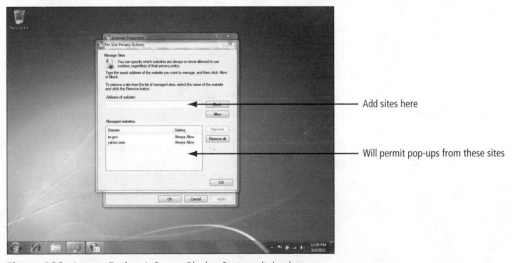

Add sites here

Will permit pop-ups from these sites

Figure 123 Internet Explorer's Pop-up Blocker Settings dialog box.

prevalent methods of spreading spyware is through file-sharing services. Not only can the file-sharing software include spyware, but often the files you think you are downloading for free are infected, too. Although it's tempting to get the newest song or video for free from such a site, don't risk it!

This problem can be avoided if you use one of the legitimate, pay-as-you-go file-sharing services such as iTunes or the reincarnated Napster. Do not trust files or software sent by friends or acquaintances. Additionally, be cautious when you download and install freeware or shareware software. Make sure you deal with a reputable software publisher, scan the downloaded software for viruses and spyware, and read the licensing agreement. Some licensing agreements actually include information about additional software that will be automatically installed if you accept it.

Another way to prevent spyware is to avoid pop-up and banner ads whenever possible. You should never click on them. Often the "No Thanks" button is just a ruse to get you to click it and enable the spyware installation. Close pop-up ads by clicking the Close button in the top right corner. Installing pop-up blocking software can help to eliminate this risk almost entirely.

If you are running the most recent version of Windows, you already have a pop-up blocker available to you as shown in **Figure 123**. You can view the pop-up blocker settings for

■ **Continue to the next page to complete the objective.**

Windows 7, as shown in **Figure 124**, and access this dialog box through Internet Explorer's Tools menu. It is also wise to avoid questionable websites, because some of them can install malware on your system just by visiting the site.

Protecting Yourself and Your Computer

There are a variety of computer security products available. Unfortunately, there are also a lot of dishonest companies purporting to offer these products. Too often, these are really scams that will actually install spyware or viruses on your system! To avoid being scammed or downloading something malicious, you should never respond to offers that are received in a pop-up ad or unsolicited email. To obtain legitimate products, it is best to purchase them from the manufacturer's website or from a local retailer. Additionally, some Internet service providers are beginning to provide some of these products as part of their services. **Figure 125** highlights some measures you can take to protect you computer from malware.

■ **Continue to the next page to complete the objective.** ➤

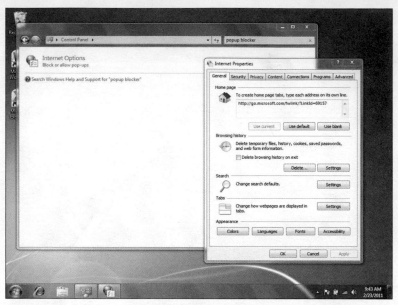

Figure 124   Popup blocker for Windows 7 is located in the Internet Properties dialog box on the Privacy tab.

Software updates and patches	Keeping your operating system and software up to date is critical. Software manufacturers are constantly on the lookout for security threats, and they issue updates and patches to help protect your system. Check for these and install them regularly. Software manufacturers have begun to implement automated procedures to check and install such updates. If your computer has this capability, it's a good idea to use this feature.
Security software	Antivirus software is a utility program used to search your hard drive and files for viruses and remove those that are found. Antispyware software works in a similar fashion, but searches for spyware rather than viruses. No computer should be without this protection. Many users erroneously think that because they aren't regularly online or use only a slow dial-up connection, they aren't a target. Nothing could be further from the truth! Recent studies show more than two-thirds of all computer users have some form of virus or spyware on their system.

Figure 125   Protection from viruses and spyware.

Some Well-Known Antivirus Products	
Norton AntiVirus	www.symantec.com
McAfee VirusScan	www.mcafee.com
AVG Anti-Virus	www.grisoft.com
Kaspersky	www.kaspersky.com
You Can Search for Other Products at Popular Download Sites Such as:	
Download.com	www.download.com
Tucows	www.tucows.com

Figure 126 Anti-Virus Products—*Note:* be sure to read the software reviews and evaluate their usefulness before downloading or installing them.

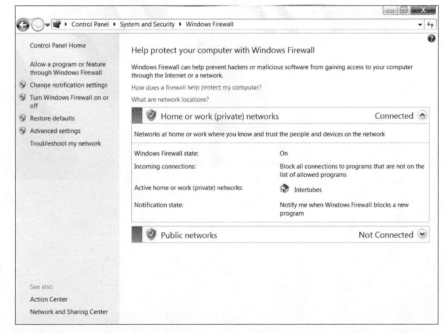

Figure 127 Software firewalls, such as the one included with Windows 7, help protect home networks from hackers.

However, it is not enough to install anti-virus software on your system; it must be updated at least once a week to check for updates. You can either run a check manually or set the software to run a check at the same time each week.

Doing so will protect you against any new viruses or malware created since the last time you checked. Software should be set to scan incoming data files, email, and so on, but regular full-system scans should be conducted on a weekly basis as well.

- *Personal firewalls—Firewalls* may be software programs, as shown in **Figure 127**, or hardware devices, although their purpose is the same—prevent unauthorized access to your computer. When a firewall is installed properly, it can close ports in order to prevent hackers from exploiting them. Not only can a good firewall help prevent infections and identity theft; it

■ **Continue to the next page to complete the objective.**

can also prevent hackers from accessing your computer and turning it into a *zombie*. A zombie computer is one that can be controlled remotely and can be used to help spread viruses, spyware, or junk email known as spam. Zombie computers can also be used in *denial of service (DoS)* attacks as shown in **Figure 128**. DoS attacks occur when a large number of computers try to access a website at the same time, effectively overloading it and causing it to shut down. If you are using Windows 7 or Windows Vista, you already have a firewall available to you.

You can access the firewall settings by clicking the Start button, settings, Control Panel, Security, and Windows Firewall.

What else should I look for? It might sound simple, but when online, do not give out personal information unless it is for legitimate purposes. It is important to avoid spam e-mail and *phishing* attacks e-mails that masquerade as authentic entities, such as banks and credit card companies, and ask for confidential information. Legitimate organizations will not ask for passwords, bank account numbers, or credit card details through e-mail. It is also possible to check for hoaxes and scams at a variety of websites, including many of the antivirus and antispyware sites. When in doubt, do some research to see if the request you've received is legitimate. If necessary, make a telephone call to the agency in question. Viewing such requests with a critical eye can help you avoid online scams and hoaxes.

Done! You have completed Objective 6 of 6.

Figure 128   Zombie computers are used to facilitate a distributed denial-of-service (DDoS) attack.

Summary

In this chapter, you examined the benefits of becoming computer competent and identified the four basic functions of computing. You explored the various types of computers and their components, including CPUs, RAM, and storage devices. This chapter also discussed how to evaluate a computer system and understand the terminology used to measure storage capacity, memory, and microprocessor speed. Various hardware and peripheral devices were reviewed, including input and output devices and different types of storage devices and media. You explored the basic types of computer software system software and application software and the different uses for each type. You identified various types of networks and the different ways networks can be configured. You also reviewed ways to maintain your computer and keep it safe from various threats, including viruses and spyware.

Key Terms

Online Help Skills

1. **Start** your web browser, for example, Internet Explorer. In the **Address Bar,** type http://windows.microsoft.com/en-US/windows-vista/Security-and-privacy-features-in-Internet-Explorer and then press ENTER. If necessary, in the upper right corner of the window, click the Maximize button.

2. Toward the middle of the page, click How can I protect my privacy when I'm online? A list of features that can help protect your privacy when online displays.

3. Read through the features and then click on Change Internet Explorer Privacy settings. Compare your screen with **Figure 1**.

4. Read the various topics and draft a short letter to a friend telling them how they can protect their privacy while online.

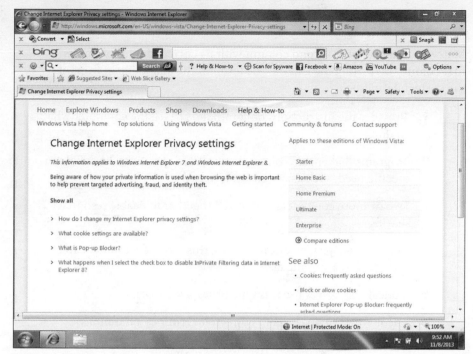

Figure 1

Matching

Match each term in the second column with its correct definition in the first column by writing the letter of the term on the blank line in front of the correct definition.

_____ **1.** Provides the instructions or commands to tell the computer what to do.

_____ **2.** Programs that enable you to accomplish a specific tasks or solve a specific need, such as Microsoft office.

_____ **3.** Two or more computers connected together to enable resource sharing.

_____ **4.** Used to manage network resources, this type of computer can be dedicated to a specific task.

_____ **5.** Optical disk drives use this type of storage media.

_____ **6.** The number of pixels on the screen determines a monitor's sharpness and clarity.

_____ **7.** A peripheral device uses this to attach to the computer.

_____ **8.** A programmable electronic device that can input, process, output, and store data.

_____ **9.** The physical components of a computer system.

_____**10.** Hardware connected outside the computer's system unit.

_____**11.** The hardware unit that typically contains the motherboard, CPU, RAM, a hard disk, and a power supply.

_____**12.** A large printed circuit board to which all the other components are connected.

_____**13.** The temporary storage that holds data and instructions waiting to be processed.

_____**14.** The processing unit.

_____**15.** This type of program threatens a user's privacy.

A. Application software

B. Computer

C. Computer network

D. Console/system unit

E. CPU

F. Hardware

G. DVDs or CDs

H. Memory (RAM)

I. Motherboard/system board

J. Peripherals

K. Port

L. Server

M. Software

N. Spyware

O. Resolution

Multiple Choice

Circle the correct response.

1. Which of the following requires one byte of storage?
   a. Page **b.** Paragraph **c.** Sentence **d.** Character

2. Which of the following units represents the fastest CPU clock speed?
   a. 733 MHz **b.** 286 MHz **c.** 2 GHz **d.** 2 GB

3. Which of the following is not an input device?
   a. Keyboard **b.** Speaker **c.** Mouse **d.** Stylus

4. Which of the following is an example of optical storage media?
   a. Disk drive **b.** Flash card **c.** RAM **d.** Compact disc

5. Which of the following is not a type of computer?
   a. Mainframe **b.** Multitask **c.** Server **d.** Supercomputer

6. Before a computer can process data, where must data be stored?
   a. In RAM **b.** On a disk **c.** In the control **d.** On the monitor unit

7. What term, related to computers, means billions?
   a. Byte **b.** Mega **c.** Giga **d.** Hertz

8. Which of the following is not a type of microcomputer?
   a. Desktop **b.** Notebook **c.** Personal digital assistant **d.** Microprocessor

9. Which of the following can prevent the easy and casual connection to your computer by a nonauthorized user?
   a. Disk defragmenter **b.** Antivirus software **c.** Firewall **d.** Key logger

10. Which of the following is capable of opening a "back door" on a computer and is able to spread without human interaction?
    a. Trojan horse **b.** Worm **c.** Adware **d.** Zombie

CHAPTER 2

Browse with Internet Explorer

- You can use Internet Explorer to browse the millions of web pages on the World Wide Web.
- Most websites provide navigation aids for finding the information at their site.
- When you are not sure where to find information, you can use special services that search the web for you.
- You can keep a list of your favorite sites and return to them with a single click. You can also revisit sites by viewing them in a list of recently visited sites.

- When you need to print a web page, you can often find a version of the page that is optimized for printing. You can also select part of the page and then print just that selection.
- Internet Explorer has several features that protect your online safety. These features can be adjusted to better meet your personal needs.

Aspen Falls City Hall

In this chapter, you will use Internet Explorer to conduct research for the Aspen Falls City Hall, which provides essential services for the citizens and visitors of Aspen Falls, California. You will locate information about area parks for Todd Austin, Tourism Director.

You will search and navigate several web sites, open sites in multiple tabs, and organize a list of favorite sites. You will also use Internet Explorer to protect your online privacy and security while you browse the web.

**Time to complete all
10 skills – 60 to 90 minutes**

Student data file needed for this chapter:

New blank WordPad document

You will save your files as:

Lastname_Firstname_ie9_01_Redwoods
Lastname_Firstname_ie9_01_Redwoods_MHT

Outcome

Using the skills in this chapter, you will be able to locate
and view websites like this:

SKILLS

**At the end of this chapter, you will
be able to:**

Skill 1   Browse the Web and Add Favorites

Skill 2   Navigate and Search Websites

Skill 3   Use Accelerators and Search Providers

Skill 4   Manage Browser Tabs

Skill 5   Organize Favorites

Skill 6   Print and Save Web Pages

Skill 7   View and Delete Browsing History

Skill 8   Protect Online Privacy

Skill 9   Change Internet Security Settings

Skill 10 Manage Pop-ups and Check Website Safety

MORE SKILLS

Skill 11 Change Your Home Page

Skill 12 Manage Search Providers

Skill 13 Manage Accelerators

Skill 14 Add Tracking Protection

▶ The *Internet* is a global collection of networks that facilitate electronic communication such as e-mail, file sharing, and the World Wide Web.

▶ *Internet Explorer* is a program used to browse the *World Wide Web*. Also known as *WWW* and the *web*, it is a collection of linked pages designed to be viewed from any computer connected to the Internet.

▶ Programs used to navigate the World Wide Web are called *web browsers*.

1. **Start** 🌐 Internet Explorer. If necessary, **Maximize** 🔲 the window.

2. Below the browser window title bar, click in the Address bar to select the text, and then compare your screen with **Figure 1**.

   When you start Internet Explorer, the page that displays is called the ***default home page***. Each Windows 7 user can set his or her own default home page.

   The Address bar, tabs, and command bar display in a single row at the top of the window.

3. With the text still selected, type us and then compare your screen with **Figure 2**.

   The text *usa.gov* is a ***domain name***—a unique name assigned to a website on the World Wide Web. The text *http://* will be inserted automatically before the domain name.

   When you type in the Address bar, the Address bar Autocomplete list displays. The websites that display in this list are based on your past browsing actions. You can navigate to these sites by clicking them.

   ■ **Continue to the next page to complete the skill**

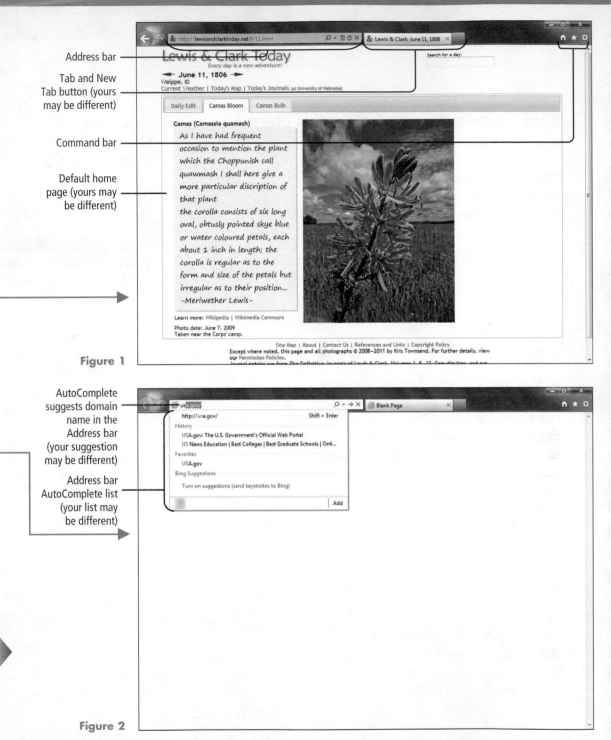

Address bar

Tab and New Tab button (yours may be different)

Command bar

Default home page (yours may be different)

Figure 1

AutoComplete suggests domain name in the Address bar (your suggestion may be different)

Address bar AutoComplete list (your list may be different)

Figure 2

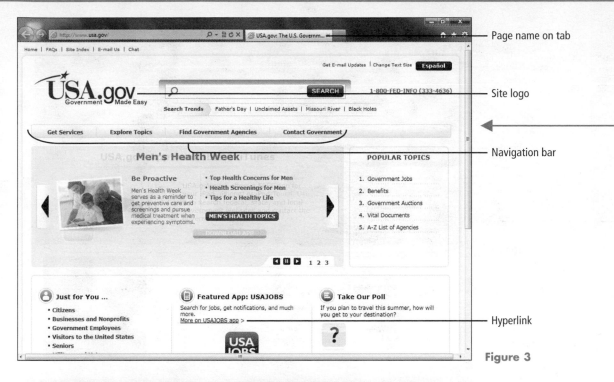

Page name on tab

Site logo

Navigation bar

Hyperlink

Figure 3

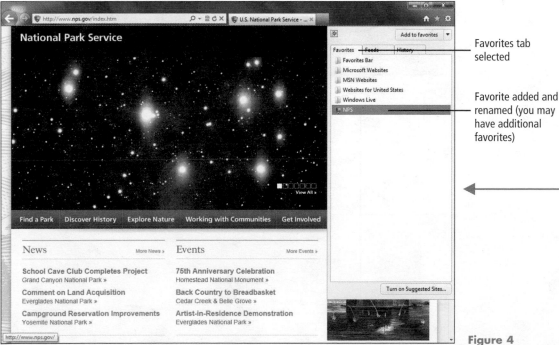

Favorites tab selected

Favorite added and renamed (you may have additional favorites)

Figure 4

4. Finish typing the domain name usa.gov and then press Enter to display the USA.gov *home page*—the starting point for the remainder of the pages at a website. Take a few moments to familiarize yourself with the features of the page, as described in **Figure 3**.

   Web pages display their domain name in the Address bar and more descriptive text on the page tab. Because the web is dynamic, the pages you see on screen may be different than the pages shown in the figures.

   The middle of the page displays *hyperlinks*—any text or pictures that can be clicked to move to a new page or location.

   Most web pages have a *navigation bar* with hyperlinks to the main pages of the site. Here, the page has a horizontal navigation bar that spans across the page.

5. Click in the Address bar, replace the text with www.nps.gov and then press Enter to navigate to the National Park Service home page.

6. On the command bar, click the **Favorites** button ⭐, and then in the **Favorites Center** that displays, click the **Add to favorites** button. In the **Add a Favorite** dialog box, in the **Name** box, replace the text with NPS and then click the **Add** button.

7. Click the **Favorites** button ⭐, click the **Favorites tab**, and then compare your screen with **Figure 4**.

   A *favorite* is a stored web address that can be clicked to navigate to that page quickly.

8. Click the **Favorites** button ⭐ to close the Favorites Center.

   ■ **You have completed Skill 1 of 10**

► A *website* is a collection of connected pages located at a single domain name. Large websites can consist of hundreds, or even thousands, of individual pages.

► Large websites provide navigation bars, hyperlinks, and their own search boxes, all of which you can use to find the pages you need.

1. In **Internet Explorer**, take a few moments to familiarize yourself with the National Park Service home page, as shown in **Figure 1**.

   Most web page headers contain the common tools for navigating the site. Here, the header has two search boxes. Below that page header, a horizontal navigation bar has links to major pages provided at this site.

2. Scroll to the bottom of the page to view the page content and display the page footer.

   Web page footers typically provide links to a site index, copyright information, and a link to contact the organization.

3. In the page footer, click the **Site Index** hyperlink to display a page that outlines the site. Compare your screen with **Figure 2**.

   A *site index*—sometimes called a *site map*—is a page of hyperlinks that outline a website.

4. On the **Site Index** page, click the **About Us** hyperlink. If that link is no longer available, click a different link.

   Because most websites are updated frequently, the pages displayed in this chapter may be different. When appropriate, substitute similar links to perform each skill.

   ■ **Continue to the next page to complete the skill**

Search boxes ──

Page header ──

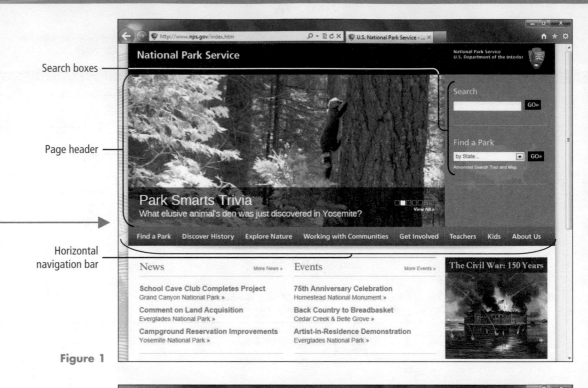

Horizontal navigation bar ──

Figure 1

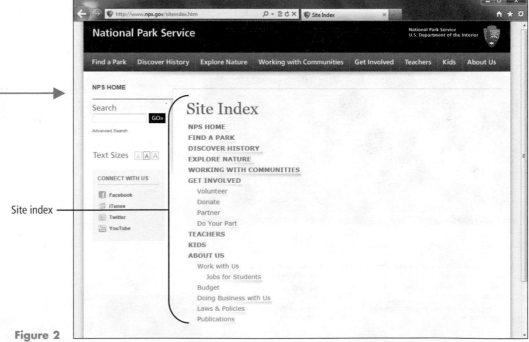

Site index ──

Figure 2

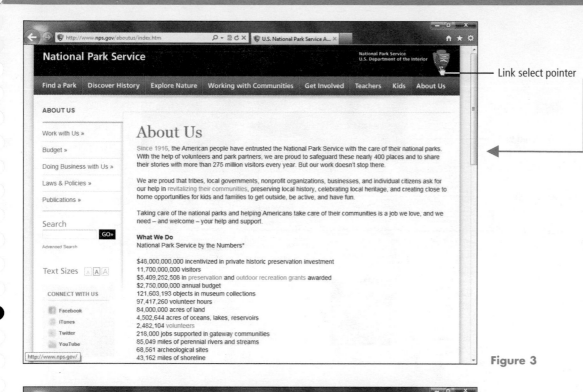

Link select pointer

Figure 3

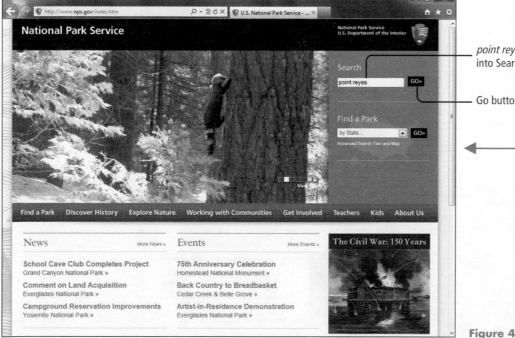

point reyes entered into Search box

Go button

Figure 4

5. In the upper right corner of the page header, point to the **National Park Service** logo to display the link select pointer, as shown in **Figure 3**.

   The 🖑 pointer displays whenever you point to a hyperlink. Clicking a site logo typically takes you to the site's home page.

6. With the 🖑 pointer displayed, click the logo to return to the site's home page.

7. On the home page, click in the upper search box, and then type point reyes Compare your screen with **Figure 4**, and then click the **Go** button.

   Many websites provide a way for you to search the site. Here, the search looks for pages about Point Reyes located on the National Park service website.

8. In the page of search results, click the **Point Reyes National Seashore (U.S. National Park Service)** hyperlink. Alternately, in the Address bar, type www.nps.gov/pore and then press Enter.

9. Click the **Favorites** button ⭐, and then click **Add to favorites**. In the **Add a Favorite** dialog box, replace the text with Point Reyes and then click the **Add** button.

10. Click the site logo to return to the home page, and leave Internet Explorer open for the next skill.

   ■ **You have completed Skill 2 of 10**

► An *Accelerator* is a feature that searches the web for information related to the text you select.

► A *search provider* is a website that provides a way for you to search the World Wide Web.

1. Click the **Favorites** button ⭐, and then in the **Favorites Center**, click **Point Reyes**.

2. In the heading *Welcome to Point Reyes National Seashore*, drag through the word *Point Reyes* to select the text. Click the **Accelerator** button 🔲 that displays, and then compare your screen with **Figure 1**.

3. In the **Accelerators** list, click **Map with Bing** to display a map of Point Reyes in a new tab. If necessary, point to **All Accelerators**, and then click **Map with Bing**.

> When you click an Accelerator, the page typically opens in a new tab. *Tabbed browsing* is a feature you use to open multiple web pages in the same browser window. Each page can be viewed by clicking its tab.

4. Click the first tab starting *Point Reyes National*. In the Address bar, click the **Show Address bar Autocomplete arrow**, and then compare your screen with **Figure 2**.

> The bottom row of the Address bar Autocomplete list displays icons for the search providers that have been added to Internet Explorer on your computer. Internet Explorer's default search provider is *Bing*. If Bing is not your default search provider, you can search with Bing by clicking its icon after entering a search term in the Address bar.

■ **Continue to the next page to complete the skill** ➤

Selected text —

Accelerator button —

Accelerators list —

Figure 1

Address bar AutoComplete arrow —

Search providers (yours may be different) —

Add search providers button —

Figure 2

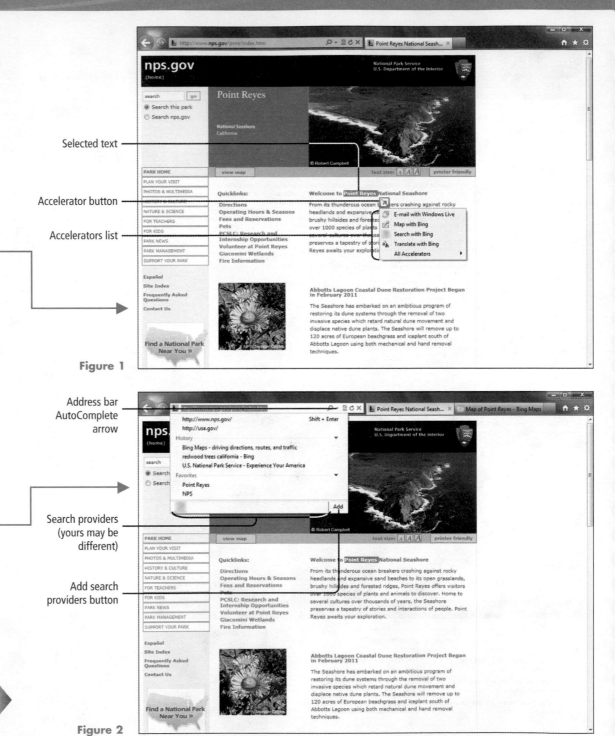

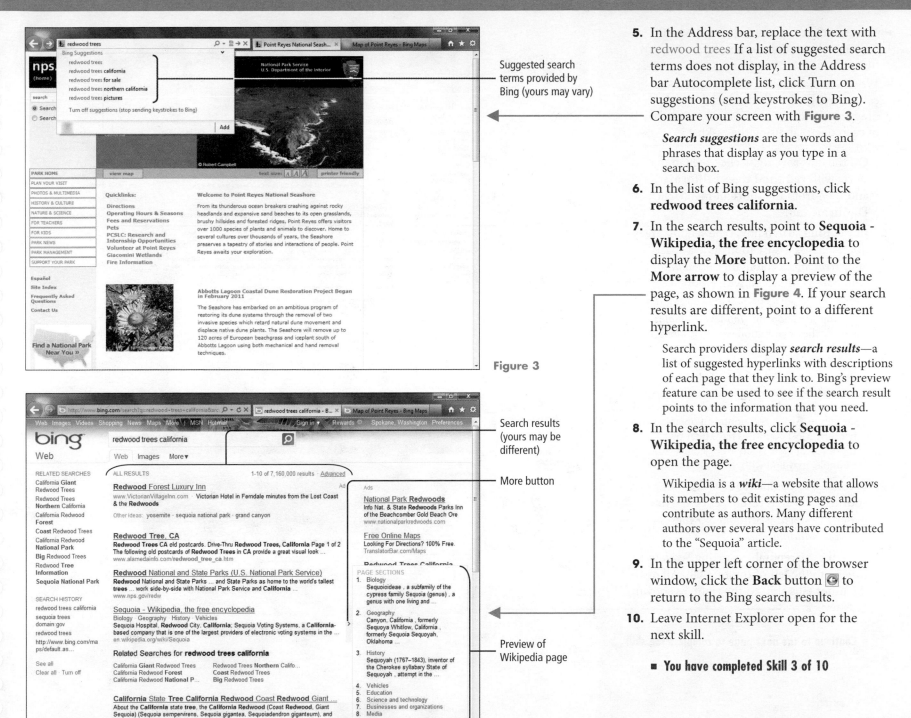

Figure 3

Figure 4

Suggested search terms provided by Bing (yours may vary)

Search results (yours may be different)

More button

Preview of Wikipedia page

5. In the Address bar, replace the text with redwood trees If a list of suggested search terms does not display, in the Address bar Autocomplete list, click Turn on suggestions (send keystrokes to Bing). Compare your screen with **Figure 3**.

   Search suggestions are the words and phrases that display as you type in a search box.

6. In the list of Bing suggestions, click **redwood trees california**.

7. In the search results, point to **Sequoia - Wikipedia, the free encyclopedia** to display the **More** button. Point to the **More arrow** to display a preview of the page, as shown in **Figure 4**. If your search results are different, point to a different hyperlink.

   Search providers display *search results*—a list of suggested hyperlinks with descriptions of each page that they link to. Bing's preview feature can be used to see if the search result points to the information that you need.

8. In the search results, click **Sequoia - Wikipedia, the free encyclopedia** to open the page.

   Wikipedia is a *wiki*—a website that allows its members to edit existing pages and contribute as authors. Many different authors over several years have contributed to the "Sequoia" article.

9. In the upper left corner of the browser window, click the **Back** button to return to the Bing search results.

10. Leave Internet Explorer open for the next skill.

   ■ **You have completed Skill 3 of 10**

► You can use a keyboard shortcut when clicking a hyperlink so that the page opens in a new tab.

► When you have multiple tabs open, you can rearrange the tabs in the tab row by dragging them. You can also view thumbnails of each open tab using the taskbar.

1. On the tabs row, right-click the tab that starts with **redwood trees california**, and then from the shortcut menu, click **Duplicate tab**.

2. In the **Bing** search box, type sequoia trees domain:gov Be sure to include a space after *trees* and a colon after *domain*. Compare your screen with **Figure 1**. ——————

The search will be limited to sites with the *gov* top-level domain. ***Top-level domains*** specify the organization type that sponsors a website and follow the period—often pronounced as *dot*—after a website's domain name. For example, federal and state government agencies use *.gov*, educational institutions use *.edu*, commercial entities use *.com*, and nonprofit organizations use *.org*. Most countries have their own top-level domain. A site from France, for example, may end with *.fr*.

3. Press Enter to complete the search. In your list of search results, click the first hyperlink starting *Sequoia & Kings Canyon National Park*.

4. Drag the current tab—starting *Sequoia & Kings*—to the left of the first tab. All of the other tabs shift to the right, as shown in **Figure 2**. ——————

■ **Continue to the next page to complete the skill** ▶

Top-level domain added to search term

Duplicated tab

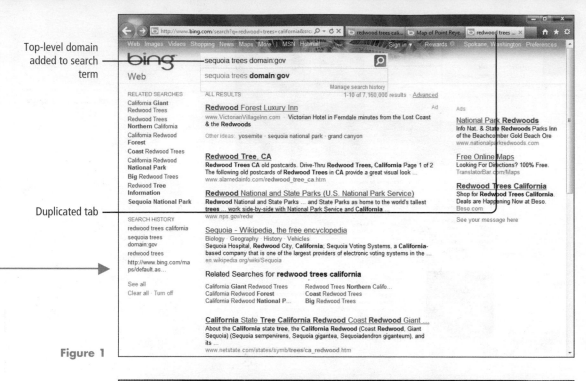

Figure 1

Tab will move to first tab position

Figure 2

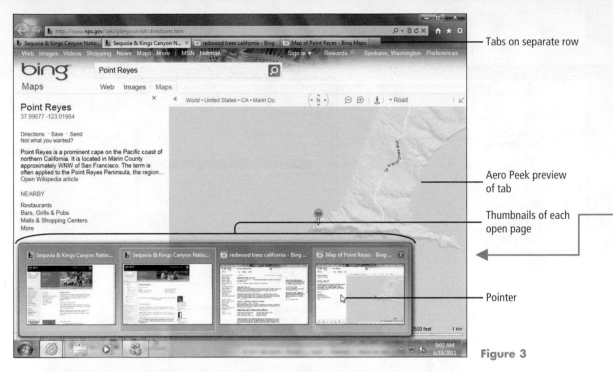

Tabs on separate row

Aero Peek preview of tab

Thumbnails of each open page

Pointer

Figure 3

5. While holding `Shift` and `Ctrl`, on the web page under **Quicklinks**, click the **Directions** hyperlink to open the page in a new tab.

6. Right-click a tab, and then from the shortcut menu, click so that the **Show tabs on a separate row** is selected (checked).

7. On the taskbar, point to the **Internet Explorer** button 🌐 to display thumbnails of each page. Point to the **Map of Point Reyes** thumbnail, and then compare your screen with **Figure 3**.

8. On the tabs row, point the **New Tab** button to display the ▫ icon. Click the **New Tab** button ▫ to open a new tab.

9. Click the **Favorites** button, and then click **Point Reyes**. On the web page, under **Quicklinks**, click **Operating Hours & Seasons**.

10. Click the **Favorites** button ⭐, and then click the **Add to favorites button arrow**. In the **Add to Favorites** list, click **Add current tabs to favorites**.

11. In the **Add Tabs to Favorites** dialog box, in the **Folder Name** box, type Redwood Research Compare your screen with **Figure 4**, and then click the **Add** button.

12. In the upper right corner of the **Internet Explorer** window, click the **Close** button ❎.

    When closing the browser with multiple tabs open, a message box will ask if you want to close the current tab or all the open tabs.

13. In the **Internet Explorer** message, click the **Close all tabs** button to exit Internet Explorer.

■ **You have completed Skill 4 of 10**

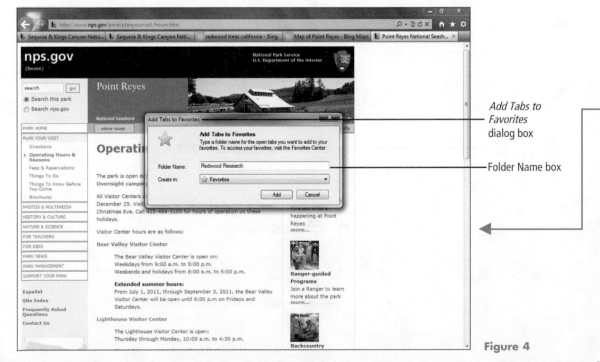

Add Tabs to Favorites dialog box

Folder Name box

Figure 4

► Over time, your list of favorites may be quite long and may need to be organized.

1. **Start** ⬤ Internet Explorer.

2. Click the **favorites** button ⭐, click the **Add to favorites button arrow**, and then at the bottom of the list, click **Organize favorites**. Click the **Point Reyes** favorite to select it, and then compare your screen with **Figure 1**.

   Information about the selected favorite displays, including its *URL*—the unique address of a page on the Internet and an acronym for *Uniform Resource Locator*.

3. With **Point Reyes** selected, click the **Delete** button to remove the favorite.

4. Click the **NPS** favorite, and then click the **Rename** button.

5. With the favorite in edit mode, type NPS Home Page and then press [Enter] to accept the change.

6. Drag the **NPS Home Page** favorite to the **Redwood Research** folder. When the **Redwood Research** folder is highlighted and the 📑 pointer displays, as shown in **Figure 2**, release the mouse button.

7. If necessary, click the Redwood Research folder to select it. Click the **Move** button. In the **Browse For Folder** dialog box, click the **Favorites Bar** folder, and then click **OK**.

   ■ **Continue to the next page to complete the skill**

Organize Favorites dialog box

Favorites list (yours may be different)

URL of selected favorite

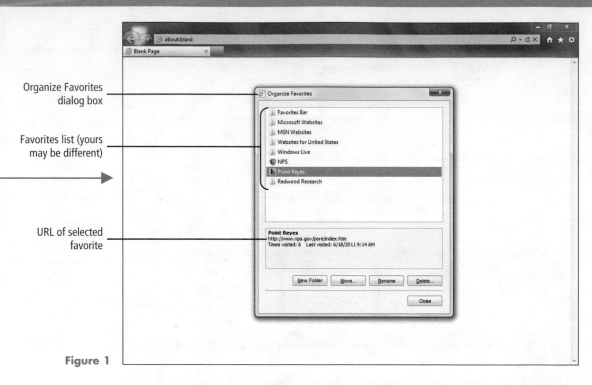

Figure 1

Favorite will be moved to folder

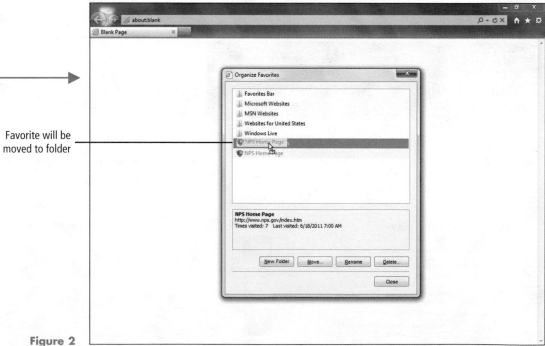

Figure 2

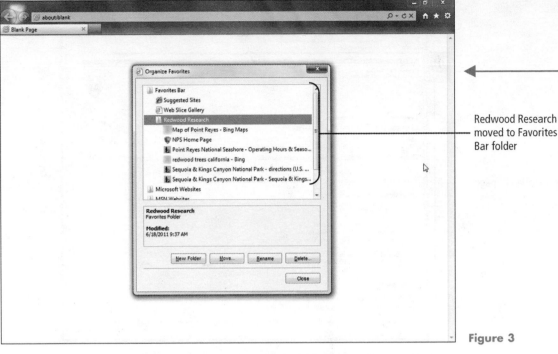

Redwood Research
moved to Favorites
Bar folder

Figure 3

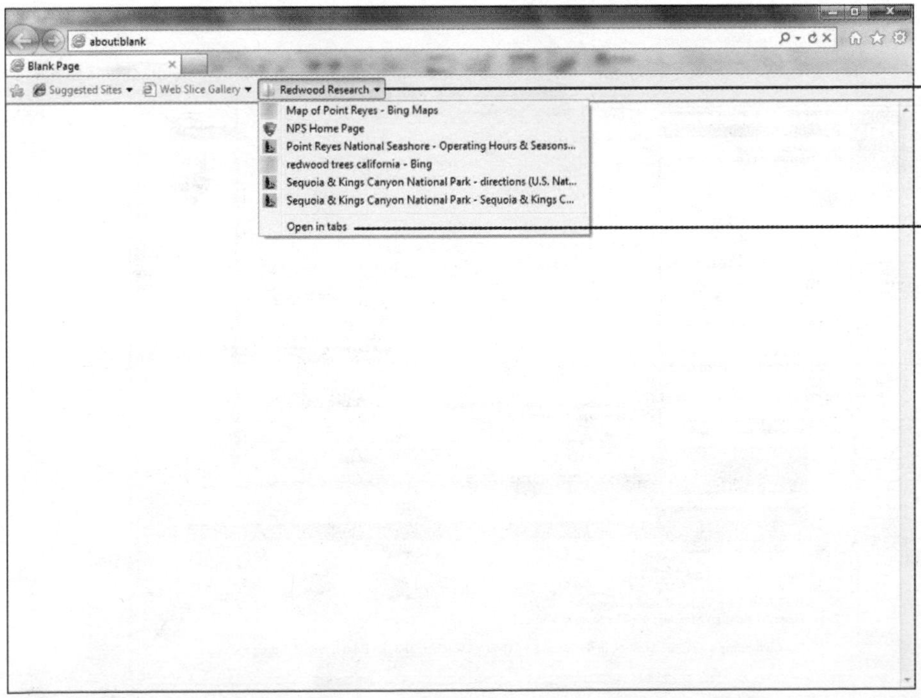

Redwood Research
on Favorites bar

Open in tabs
command

Figure 4

8. In the **Organize Favorites** dialog box, click the **Favorites Bar** folder, and then click the **Redwood Research** folder to display its list. Compare your screen with **Figure 3**.

9. Create a **Full-screen Snip**. **Copy** 🗎 the snip, and then **Close** ❎ the markup window without saving the changes.

10. **Start** WordPad. Type your first and last name, press Enter, and then type IE 9 Chapter 2 Skills 1-10

11. Press Enter, and then **Paste** the snip. Press Enter, and then type Redwood Research favorites

12. Click **Save** 💾. In the **Save As** dialog box, display your **USB flash drive** file list, and then click the **New folder** button. Type Internet Explorer 9 Chapter 2 and then press Enter two times. In the **File name** box, type Lastname_Firstname_ie9_01_Redwoods and then click **Save**.

13. Switch to **Internet Explorer**. In the **Organize Favorites** dialog box, click the **Close** button.

14. Right-click a blank area in the tabs row, and then click so that **Favorites bar** is selected (checked).

15. On the Favorites bar, click the **Redwood Research** button, and then compare your screen with **Figure 4**.

   Items added to the Favorites Bar folder display on the Favorites bar. When you add a folder to the Favorites bar, it displays as a menu. You can click an individual favorite or open all of them by clicking the Open in tabs command.

16. From the **Redwood Research** list, click the favorite starting *Point Reyes National*.

■ **You have completed Skill 5 of 10**

► When you need to store information on a web page, you can print the page or save it to your drive.

1. In Internet Explorer, on the **Operating Hours & Seasons** page, below the photo, click the **printer friendly** button, and then compare your screen with **Figure 1**.

   Many sites offer *printer friendly pages*—alternate pages that are designed to be printed. Here, the navigation bar and most of the graphics have been removed.

2. Point to the left of the *Bear Valley Visitor Center* heading, and then click and drag to the right of the last word in that section—*Saturdays*.

3. Right-click the text selected in the previous step, and then from the shortcut menu, click **Print**. In the **Print** dialog box, under **Page Range**, select the **Selection** option button. Compare your screen with **Figure 2**.

   With the Selection option, only the selected information will be printed.

4. Create a **Full-screen Snip**. **Copy** 📋 the snip, and then **Close** ✖ the markup window without saving the changes.

5. Switch to **WordPad**, press Enter, and then **Paste** the snip. Press Enter, type Print Selection and then click **Save** 💾.

6. **Minimize** ➖ **WordPad**. In the **Print** dialog box, click **Cancel**, and then **Close** ✖ the printer-friendly window.

   ■ **Continue to the next page to complete the skill** ►

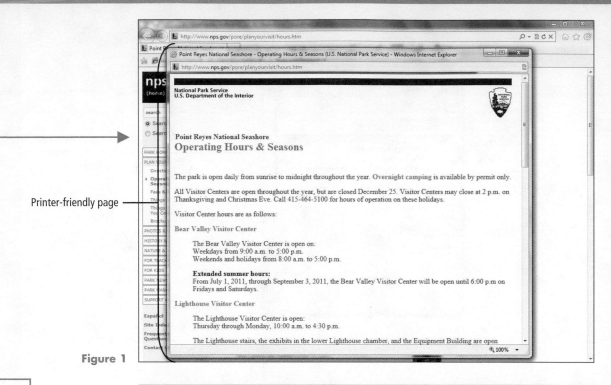

Printer-friendly page

Figure 1

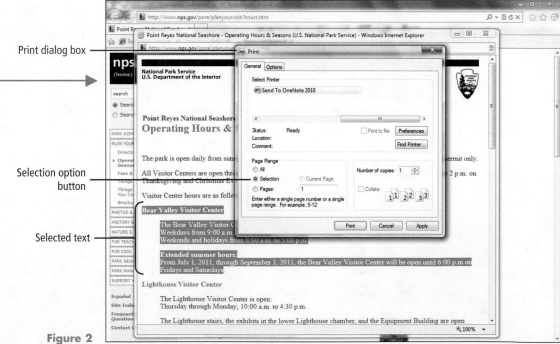

Print dialog box

Selection option button

Selected text

Figure 2

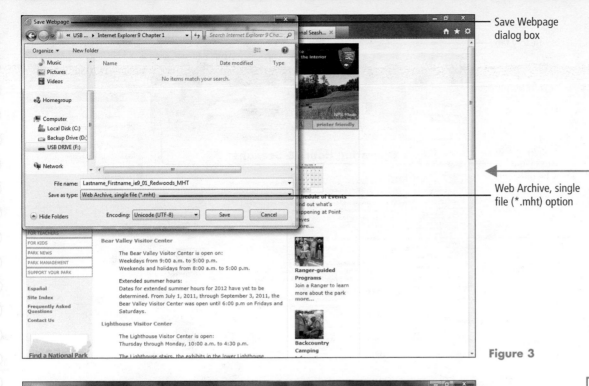

Save Webpage dialog box

Web Archive, single file (*.mht) option

Figure 3

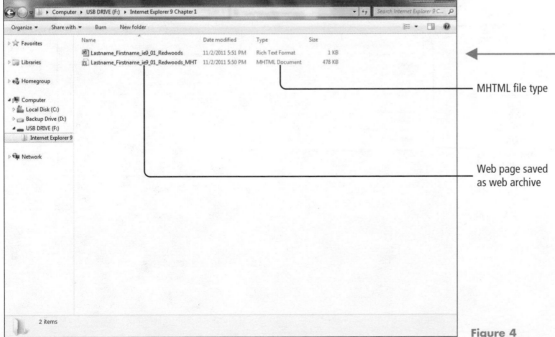

MHTML file type

Web page saved as web archive

Figure 4

7. On the command bar, click the **Tools** button ⚙, point to **File**, and then click **Save as**. In the **Save Webpage** dialog box, display your **Internet Explorer 9 Chapter 2** file list. Click in the **File name** box, and then replace the selected text with Lastname_Firstname_ie9_01_ Redwoods_MHT Click the **Save as type** button, and then click **Web Archive, single file (*.mht)**. Compare your screen with **Figure 3**.

    A *web archive* is a file that saves the web page text and its pictures in a single file. These files are typically assigned the *.mht* file extension. Web archives are also known as *MHTML files*.

8. Click **Save**, and then **Close** ⬚ Internet Explorer.

9. Click **Start** ⬡, and then click **Computer**. In the **Computer** window, navigate to your **Internet Explorer 9 Chapter 2** file list. Compare your screen with **Figure 4**.

10. In the file list, double-click **Lastname_ Firstname_ie9_01 _Redwoods_MHT** to open it in Internet Explorer.

11. **Maximize** ⬚ the Internet Explorer window. On the Favorites bar, right-click the **Redwood Research** folder. From the shortcut menu, click **Delete**. Read the displayed message, and then click **Yes** to remove the six favorites.

12. Right-click the Favorites bar, and then from the shortcut menu, click **Favorites bar** to hide the bar.

■ **You have completed Skill 6 of 10**

▶ As you browse the web, Internet Explorer stores information that helps you browse more efficiently. This information is called your ***browsing history***, which you can view and delete as desired.

1. In **Internet Explorer**, click the **Favorites** button ⭐, and then in the **Favorites Center**, click the **History tab**.

2. At the top of the **History** list, click the **View By** button, and then click **View By Site**. In the **History** list, click **bing (www.bing.com)**, and then compare your screen with **Figure 1**.

3. Click the **View By** button, and then click **View By Date**. Click **Today**, and then click **nps (www.nps.gov)** to show the National Park Service sites that you visited today. Click **Site Index** to open the page.

4. Click in the Address bar, type windowslive.com/desktop/familysafety and then press Enter.

5. **Close** ✕ Internet Explorer, and then **Close** ✕ Windows Explorer.

6. **Start** 🌐 Internet Explorer, and if necessary **Maximize** 🔲 the window. In the Address bar, select the text. Watch the **Address bar Autocomplete** list as you type windows Compare your screen with **Figure 2**.

   As you type in the Address bar, your history list displays a list of sites that you have visited that match what you are typing. In Figure 2, the Family Safety page displayed at the top of the list after typing the first three characters—*win*. Depending on your history, you may need to type more of the address.

■ **Continue to the next page to complete the skill** ▶

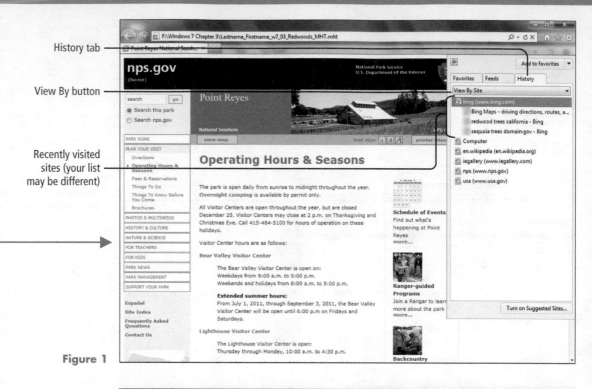

History tab

View By button

Recently visited sites (your list may be different)

Figure 1

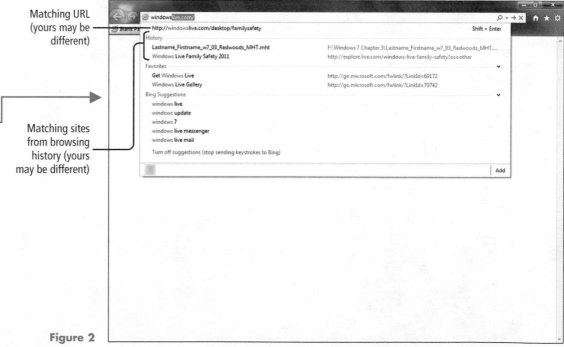

Matching URL (yours may be different)

Matching sites from browsing history (yours may be different)

Figure 2

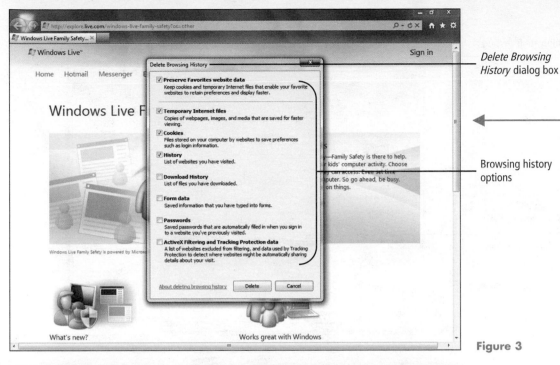

Delete Browsing History dialog box

Browsing history options

Figure 3

7. In the **Address bar Autocomplete** list, click **http://windowslive.com/desktop/ familysafety** to navigate to page.

8. On the command bar, click the **Tools** button ⚙, point to **Safety**, and then click **Delete browsing history**. Compare your screen with **Figure 3**.

   In the Delete Browsing History dialog box, you can choose which portions of your browsing history to delete. The different options are summarized in **Figure 4**. When you want to delete all of your favorites, clear the Preserve Favorites website data check box.

9. Create a **Full-screen Snip**. **Copy** 🖺 the snip, and then **Close** 🔳 the markup window without saving the changes.

10. Switch to **WordPad**. Press Enter, and then **Paste** the snip. Press Enter, type Delete Browsing History and then click **Save** 🖫.

11. Switch to **Internet Explorer**. If you want to delete your browsing history, click the **Delete** button. Otherwise, click **Cancel**.

    When you are working on a *public computer*—a computer that is available to others when you are not using it—it is a good idea to delete your browsing history before logging off the computer.

■ **You have completed Skill 7 of 10**

Browsing History Settings

Browsing History Category	Purpose
Temporary Internet files	Copies of web pages and their images stored in your personal folder. These are used to improve the time that it takes for frequently visited pages to display.
Cookies	Small text files written by some websites as you visit them. They are used to add functionality to pages and to analyze the way you use a website.
History	A list of all the web pages you have visited.
Form data	Information that you have typed into forms, such as your logon name, e-mail address, and street address.
Passwords	Any logon passwords that you choose to save with Internet Explorer are stored here.
InPrivate Filtering data	Data used by InPrivate to determine if a website is sharing information about your visit.

Figure 4

► You can protect your privacy with *InPrivate Browsing*—an Internet Explorer window that limits the browsing history that is written.

► You can allow or prevent specific sites from writing cookies on your computer.

1. In **Internet Explorer**, click the **New Tab** button ⬜. At the bottom of the new page, click **InPrivate Browsing**.

2. On the **about:InPrivate** page, take a few moments to read the information about InPrivate Browsing.

3. On the taskbar, point to the **Internet Explorer** button 🌐 to display all open pages. Compare your screen with **Figure 1**. ──────

   When you start InPrivate Browsing, a new Internet Explorer window opens. InPrivate Browsing is in effect only when that window is used.

4. On the **about:InPrivate** page, in the Address bar, replace the text with nps.gov/muwo and then press⏎.

5. On the command bar, click the **Tools** button ⚙, point to **Safety**, and then click **Webpage privacy policy**. Compare your screen with **Figure 2**. ──────

   The Privacy Report tells you if a site has written cookies. Here, the InPrivate Browsing window has accepted a cookie from the Muir Woods page. Recall that cookies typically are stored in your personal folder. InPrivate writes cookies to *RAM*—a computer's temporary electronic memory. When the window is closed, the cookie is removed from RAM.

   ■ **Continue to the next page to complete the skill** ▶

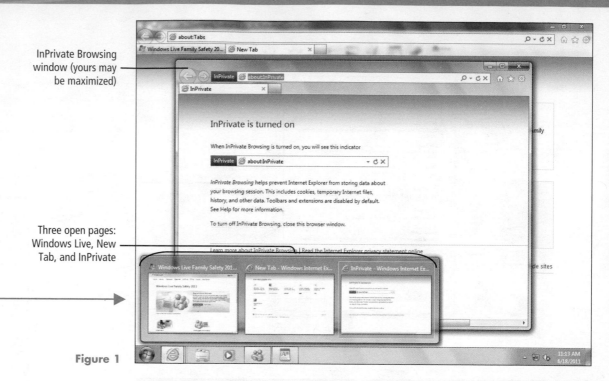

InPrivate Browsing window (yours may be maximized)

Three open pages: Windows Live, New Tab, and InPrivate

Figure 1

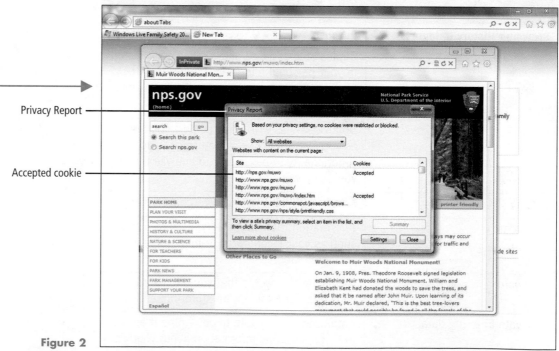

Privacy Report

Accepted cookie

Figure 2

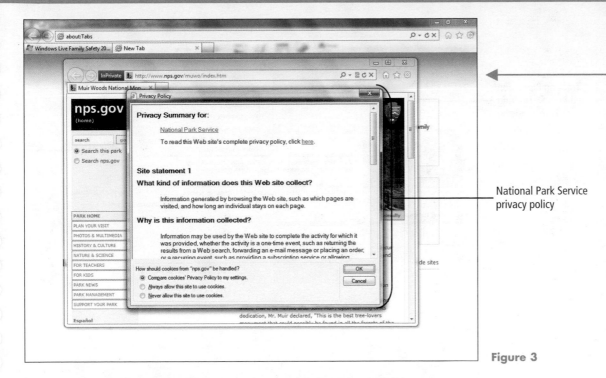

National Park Service
privacy policy

Figure 3

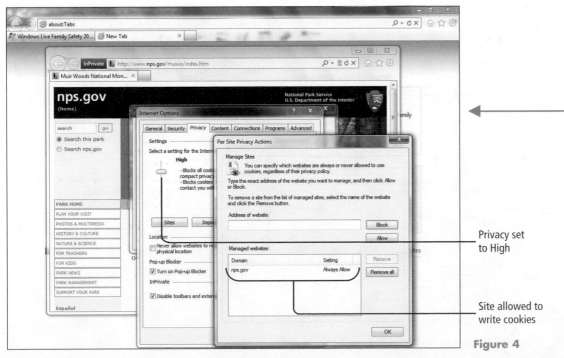

Privacy set
to High

Site allowed to
write cookies

Figure 4

6. In the **Privacy Report** dialog box, click **http://www.nps.gov/muwo/index.htm**, and then click the **Summary** button. Compare your screen with **Figure 3**.

   A *privacy policy* explains what types of information is collected and how it will be used.

7. At the bottom of the **Privacy Policy** dialog box, select the **Always allow this site to use cookies** option button.

8. Click **OK**, and then in the **Privacy Report** dialog box, click the **Settings** button. Alternately, click the Tools button 🔧, click **Internet options**, and then click the **Privacy tab**.

9. In the **Internet options** dialog box, drag the slider up to set the privacy level to **High**.

10. Click the **Sites** button, and then move the **Per Site Privacy Actions** dialog box to the right so that it does not cover the privacy setting slider. Compare your screen with **Figure 4**.

    With privacy set to high, only the sites you allow can write cookies.

11. Create a **Full-screen Snip**. **Copy** 🔲 the snip, and then click **Close** ❎.

12. In **Internet Explorer**, under **Managed websites**, click **nps.gov**, and then click **Remove**. Click **OK**, and then in the **Internet Options** dialog box, click the **Default** button to restore your original setting.

13. Click **OK**, **Close** ❎ the **Privacy Report**, and then **Close** ❎ the **InPrivate** window.

14. Switch to **WordPad**. Press ⏎, and then **Paste** the snip. **Press** ⏎, type Privacy Settings and then click **Save** 💾.

■ **You have completed Skill 8 of 10**

► Some sites use scripts and active content to download *malware*—a type of program designed to harm your computer, control your computer, or discover private information.

► *Scripts* and *active content* are programs downloaded with a web page that provide additional functionality, such as dynamic content.

1. Switch to the **New Tab** window. Click in the Address bar, type myitlab.pearsoned .com and then press Enter.

   You can use the Safety menu to control *tracking cookies*—cookies that gather information about your web browsing behaviors. You can also open an InPrivate Browsing window or filter *ActiveX scripts*— small programs that allow websites to provide content such as learning management systems.

2. On the command bar, click the **Tools** button ⚙, point to **Safety**, and then compare your screen with **Figure 1**.

3. From the **Tools** menu, click **Internet options**. In the **Internet Options** dialog box, click the **Security tab**, and then compare your screen with **Figure 2**.

   Protected Mode is a feature that makes it more difficult for malware to be installed on your computer. By default, Protected Mode is enabled in the Internet and Restricted sites zones.

   The *Local intranet* zone is designed for web content stored on internal networks that is accessed only by those within the organization. Any web page not assigned to one of the other three zones is assigned to the Internet zone.

■ **Continue to the next page to complete the skill** ▶

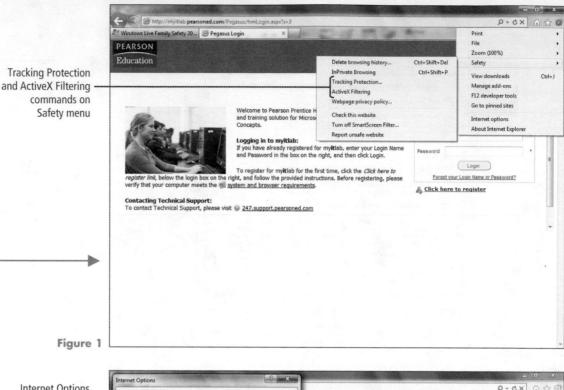

Tracking Protection and ActiveX Filtering commands on Safety menu

Figure 1

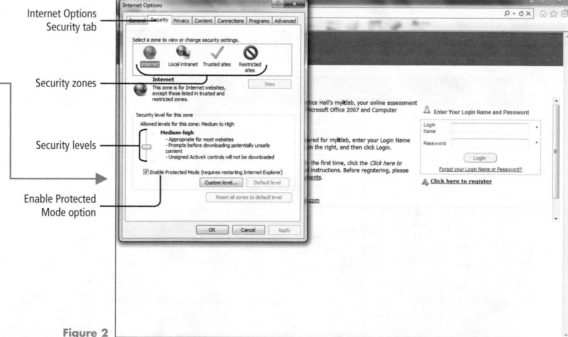

Internet Options Security tab

Security zones

Security levels

Enable Protected Mode option

Figure 2

Internet Security Levels

Level	Description
High	No file downloads, scripts, or active content allowed.
Medium-high	Files can be downloaded, but a prompt must first display for approval. Some scripts and active content are classified as unsafe and are blocked.
Medium	Files can be downloaded and a prompt displays before running any potentially unsafe scripts or active content.
Medium-low	This level is available only in the Local intranet and Trusted sites zones. A smaller range of scripts and active content is classified as unsafe.
Low	This level is available only in the Local intranet and Trusted sites zones and should be applied only to a site you absolutely trust.

Figure 3

4. In the **Internet Options** dialog box, click the **Trusted sites** icon. Note your current security level for this zone. The security levels are summarized in the table in **Figure 3**.

   Each security zone has its own security level. For example, any site added to Restricted sites is prevented from running scripts or active content. By default, the Trusted sites zone is set to Mcdium. Some websites will not work properly unless they are added to Trusted sites.

5. Click the **Sites** button. In the **Trusted sites** dialog box, clear the **Require server verification (https:) for all sites in this zone** check box, and then click **Add** to add the current site to the Trusted sites zone. Compare your screen with **Figure 4**.

   MyITLab is a site you can trust to run active content in a safe and secure manner.

6. Create a **Full-screen Snip**. **Copy** the snip, and then click **Close** without saving changes.

7. In the **Trusted sites** dialog box, click **http://myitlab.pearsoned.com**, and then click the **Remove** button. Click the **Close** button, and then in the **Internet Options** dialog box, click **Cancel**.

8. Switch to **WordPad**. Press [Enter], and then **Paste** the snip. Press [Enter], type Trusted Sites and then click **Save**.

9. Switch to the **Pegasus Login** window, and leave Internet Explorer open for the next skill.

   ■ **You have completed Skill 9 of 10**

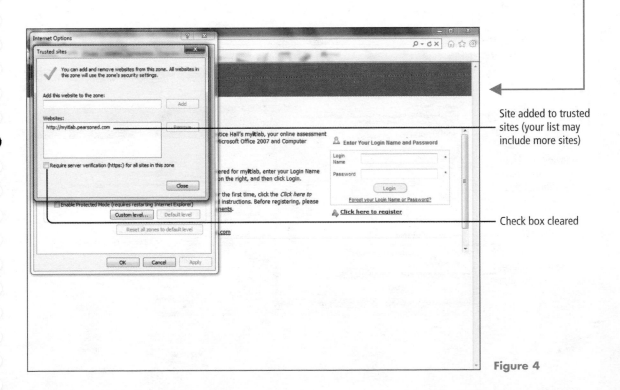

Site added to trusted sites (your list may include more sites)

Check box cleared

Figure 4

▶ *Pop-ups* are small windows that display in addition to the web page you are viewing.

▶ *SmartScreen Filter* is a feature that helps protect you from online threats.

1. On the Internet Explorer command bar, click the **Tools** button ⚙, and then click **Internet options**. In the **Internet Options** dialog box, click the **Privacy tab**. Under **Pop-up Blocker**, click the **Settings** button, and then compare your screen with **Figure 1**.

2. In the **Pop-up Blocker Settings** dialog box, in the **Address of website to allow** box, type pearsoned.com and then click the **Add** button to move the site into **Allowed sites**.

3. Click the **Blocking level** button, and then click **High: Block all pop-ups**. Compare your screen with **Figure 2**.

   At many websites, pop-ups add functionality. However, some websites use pop-ups to display unwanted advertising. When you set the blocking level to high, only the sites you allow will be able to display pop-ups. Here, pages from pearsoned.com—such as MyITLab—will be the only pages allowed to display pop-ups.

4. Create a **Full-screen Snip**. **Copy** 📋 the snip, and then click **Close** ✖.

5. Switch to **WordPad**. Press [Enter], and then **Paste** the snip. Press [Enter], type Pop-up Blocker Settings and then click **Save** 💾.

6. Switch to **Pegasus Login** 🌐. In the **Pop-up Blocker Settings** dialog box, under **Allowed sites**, click *.**pearsoned .com**, and then click the **Remove** button.

■ **Continue to the next page to complete the skill** ▶

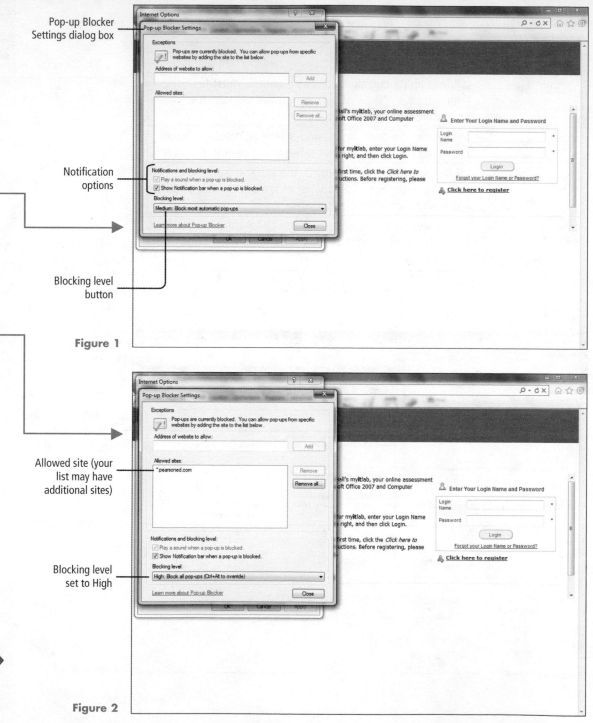

Pop-up Blocker Settings dialog box

Notification options

Blocking level button

Figure 1

Allowed site (your list may have additional sites)

Blocking level set to High

Figure 2

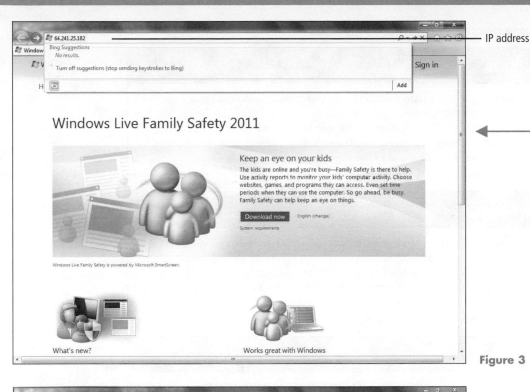

IP address

Windows Live Family Safety 2011

Keep an eye on your kids

The kids are online and you're busy—Family Safety is there to help. Use activity reports to monitor your kids' computer activity. Choose websites, games, and programs they can access. Even set time periods when they can use the computer. So go ahead, be busy. Family Safety can help keep an eye on things.

Download now   English (change)

System requirements

Windows Live Family Safety is powered by Microsoft SmartScreen.

What's new?   Works great with Windows

Figure 3

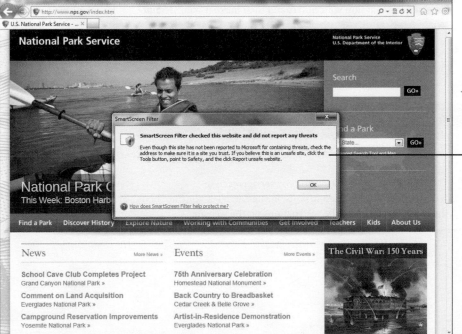

SmartScreen Filter did not find any threats

Figure 4

7. Set the **Blocking level** to **Medium: Block most automatic pop-ups**, and then close all open dialog boxes. **Close** ⊠ the tab starting *Pegasus Login*.

8. In the Address bar, type the IP address 64.241.25.182 Compare your screen with **Figure 3**, and then press Enter.

> An *IP address* is a unique set of numbers assigned to each computer on the Internet. *Phishing sites*—dishonest sites posing as legitimate sites to gain personal information, such as your logon and bank account number—often mask their identity by using an IP address instead of a URL.

9. On the command bar, click the **Tools** button ⚙, point to **Safety**, and then click **Check this website**. Compare your screen with **Figure 4**. If necessary, click **OK** to check the site.

> SmartScreen Filter maintains a list of known malicious sites and files.

10. Create a **Full-Screen Snip**. **Copy** 📄 the snip, and then click **Close** ⊠.

11. In **Internet Explorer**, click **OK**. Right-click the tabs row, and then click so that the **Show tabs on a separate row** is no longer checked. **Close** ⊠ Internet Explorer.

12. In **WordPad**, press Enter, and then **Paste** the snip. Press Enter, type SmartScreen Filter and then click **Save** 💾. If you are printing this project, print the WordPad document.

13. **Exit** WordPad, and then submit your printout or file as directed by your instructor.

Done! You have completed Skill 10 of 10

More Skills

The following More Skills are located at **www.pearsonhighered.com/skills**

More Skills 11 Change Your Home Page

Recall that when you start Internet Explorer, your default home page automatically opens. You can change the default home page to any page you want.

In More Skills 11, you will change the default home page for Internet Explorer.

To begin, open your web browser, navigate to www.pearsonhighered.com/skills, locate and click your textbook's hyperlink, and follow the instructions on the website.

More Skills 12 Manage Search Providers

In the Internet Explorer search box, you can select another search provider, or add and remove providers from the list. You can choose from hundreds of search providers, and set your favorite provider to display in the search box when you open Internet Explorer.

In More Skills 12, you will add three search providers, set a new default provider, and then search using each of the providers.

To begin, open your web browser, navigate to www.pearsonhighered.com/skills, locate and click your textbook's hyperlink, and follow the instructions on the website.

More Skills 13 Manage Accelerators

Recall that you can use Accelerators to search for information using the selected text. You can add and remove Accelerators to accomplish other tasks such as sharing information with others.

In More Skills 13, you will add an Accelerator that is used to share information with others and then make it your default share Accelerator.

To begin, open your web browser, navigate to www.pearsonhighered.com/skills, locate and click your textbook's hyperlink, and follow the instructions on the website.

More Skills 14 Add Tracking Protection

You can use Internet Explorer's safety features to prevent websites from gathering information about your web browsing behaviors.

In More Skills 14, you will add a Tracking Protection service to Internet Explorer.

To begin, open your web browser, navigate to www.pearsonhighered.com/skills, locate and click your textbook's hyperlink, and follow the instructions on the website.

Key Terms

Online Help Skills

1. **Start** your web browser, such as Internet Explorer. In the Address bar, type http://windows.microsoft.com/en-US/windows7/Getting-started-with-Internet-Explorer-9 and then press Enter to display the **Getting started with Internet Explorer 9** web page. Compare your screen with **Figure 1**.

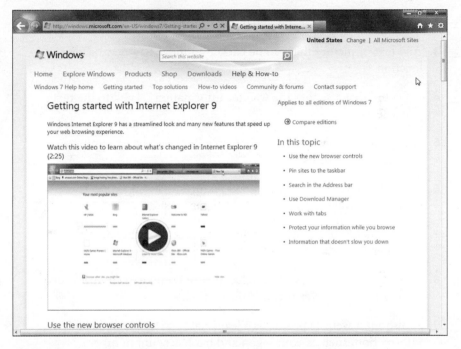

Figure 1

2. Turn on your speakers or put on headphones, and then click the **Play** button ▶. If the video does not play, you may need to follow the onscreen directions to install Microsoft Silverlight from www.silverlight.net.

3. Listen to and watch the demonstration, and then see if you can answer the following questions: When might you want to pin the Favorites Center to the left of the browser window? How can you use the New Tab button to navigate to the sites you visit most often?

Matching

Match each term in the second column with its correct definition in the first column by writing the letter of the term on the blank line in front of the correct definition.

___ **1.** A unique name assigned to a website on the World Wide Web.

___ **2.** The starting point for the remainder of the pages at a website.

___ **3.** Any text or picture that can be clicked to move to a new page or location.

___ **4.** A feature that searches the web for information related to the text you select.

___ **5.** A website that allows its members to edit existing pages and contribute as authors.

___ **6.** A file that saves web page text and pictures in a single file. These files are typically assigned the .mht file extension.

___ **7.** An Internet Explorer window that limits the browsing history that is written.

___ **8.** A type of program designed to harm your computer, control your computer, or discover private information.

___ **9.** A dishonest website posing as a legitimate site to gain personal information, such as your logon and bank account number.

___ **10.** A small window that displays in addition to the web page you are viewing.

A Accelerator

B Domain name

C Home page

D Hyperlink

E InPrivate Browsing

F Malware

G Phishing site

H Pop-up

I Web archive

J Wiki

Multiple Choice

Choose the correct answer.

1. A stored web address that can be clicked to navigate to that page quickly.
   A. Favorite
   B. Quicklink
   C. Top-level domain name

2. A vertical or horizontal bar with hyperlinks to the main pages of a website.
   A. Accelerator
   B. Navigation bar
   C. Site index

3. A collection of linked pages designed to be viewed from any computer connected to the Internet.
   A. Temporary Internet files
   B. Web archive
   C. World Wide Web

4. A website that provides a way for you to search for information on the web.
   A. Accelerator
   B. Search provider
   C. Uniform Resource Locator

5. Letters after a domain name that specify the type of organization sponsoring a website—*.gov*, for example.
   A. Cookie
   B. Top-level domain
   C. URL

6. The unique address of a page on the Internet.
   A. Site index
   B. Top-level domain
   C. URL

7. The information that Internet Explorer stores as you browse the web.
   A. Browsing History
   B. Site map
   C. Wiki

8. A program downloaded with a web page that provides additional functionality.
   A. Accelerator
   B. Active content
   C. InPrivate Browsing

9. Web content stored on internal networks that is accessed only by those within the organization.
   A. Local intranet
   B. Local network
   C. Local web

10. A unique set of numbers assigned to each computer on the Internet.
    A. Location code
    B. IP address
    C. URL

Topics for Discussion

1. Consider the websites you might visit. Which ones should be added as favorites? Of those favorites, which ones would you add to the Favorites bar?

2. In this chapter, you practiced protecting your privacy and security when you use the Internet. What websites do you think it is OK to give personal information to, and under what circumstances?

Skill Check

To complete this project, you will need the following file:

- New blank WordPad document

You will save your file as:

- Lastname_Firstname_ie9_01_Monuments

1. **Start** Internet Explorer. In the Address bar, type blm.gov and then press Enter.

2. On the **Bureau of Land Management** home page, on its vertical navigation bar, click **Visit Us**, and then from the list that displays, click **Monuments**.

3. Scroll down to display the **California** monuments, and then click the **Carrizo Plain National Monument** hyperlink.

4. Click the **Favorites** button, and then click the **Add to favorites** button. In the **Add a Favorite** dialog box, replace the suggested **Name** with Carrizo Plain and then click **Add**.

5. Scroll to the bottom of the page. In the page footer, press and hold Ctrl + Shift, while clicking the **Site Map** hyperlink to open the link in a new tab.

6. On the tab row, click the first tab—starting *Carrizo Plain*. Click the **Favorites** button, and then in the **Favorites Center**, click the **History tab**. If necessary, change to **View by Date**. Click **Today**, click **blm (www.blm.gov)**, and then click **National Monuments**.

7. Scroll to display the **California** monuments. In the second line of the second article, select the text *Carrizo Plain National Monument*. Click the **Accelerator** button, and then point to **All Accelerators**. Compare your screen with **Figure 1**, and then click **Map with Bing**.

8. Click the **New Tab** button. In the Address bar, type carrizo plain and then in the **Address bar Autocomplete** list, click the first search term suggested by Bing.

9. Click the **Favorites** button, and then click the **Add to Favorites button arrow**. In the **Add to Favorites** list, click **Add current tabs to favorites**. In the **Folder Name** box, type California Monuments and then click **Add**.

10. Click the **Favorites** button, click the **Add to Favorites button arrow**, and then click **Organize favorites**. Drag the **Carrizo Plain** favorite into the **California Monuments** folder. Click the **California Monuments** folder, and then compare your screen with **Figure 2**.

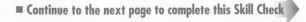

■ Continue to the next page to complete this Skill Check ▶

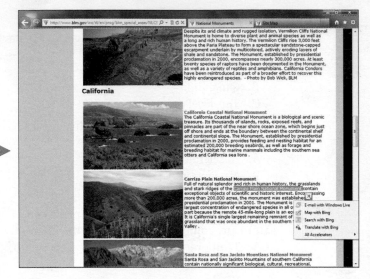

Figure 1

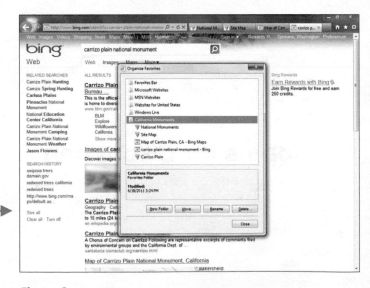

Figure 2

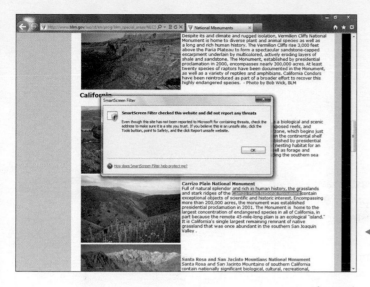

Figure 3

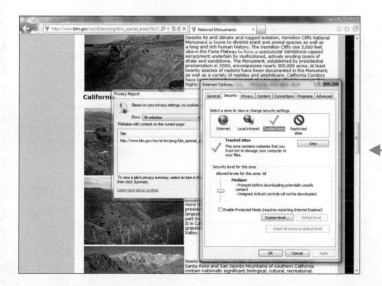

Figure 4

11. Create a **Full-screen Snip**, click **Copy**, and then **Close** the markup window without saving changes. **Start** WordPad. Type your first and last name, press Enter, and then type IE 9 Chapter 2 Skill Check

12. Create a new line, and then click **Paste**. Press Enter, and then type Favorites Center

13. Click **Save**. In the **Save As** dialog box, display your **Internet Explorer 9 Chapter 2** file list. Name the file Lastname_Firstname_ie9_01_Monuments and then click **Save**.

14. Minimize WordPad. With the **California Monuments** folder selected in the **Organize Favorites** dialog box, click the **Delete** button. Click **Yes**, and then click **Close**.

15. On the tabs row, right-click the first tab, and then in the list, click **Close other tabs**.

16. Click the **Tools** button, point to **Safety**, and then click **Check this website**. Compare your screen with **Figure 3**.

17. Create a **Full-screen Snip**, click **Copy**, and then **Close** the window without saving the changes. Click **OK**.

18. In **WordPad**, create a new line, and then click **Paste**. Press Enter, and then type SmartScreen Filter Check

19. In **SmartScreen Filter** dialog box, click **OK**. Click the **Tools** button, point to **Safety**, and then click **Webpage privacy policy**. In the **Privacy Report**, click the **Settings** button.

20. Click the **Security tab**, and then click **Trusted sites**. Move the **Internet Options** dialog box to the right, as shown in **Figure 4**.

21. Create a **Full-screen Snip**, click **Copy**, and then **Close** the window without saving the changes. In **WordPad**, create a new line, and then click **Paste**. Press Enter, and then type Privacy and Security Settings If you are printing this project, print the WordPad document. Click **Save**, and then **Exit** WordPad.

22. Switch to **Internet Explorer**, and then **Close** all open dialog boxes.

23. Below the **National Monuments** page header, click the **Print Page** hyperlink. Select the first paragraph that begins *The Bureau of Land*.

24. On the command bar, click the **Tools** button, point to **Print**, and then click **Print**. In the **Print** dialog box, under **Page Range**, select the **Selection** option button. If you are printing this project, click **Print**. Otherwise, click **Cancel**.

25. Close Internet Explorer. Submit your printout or files as directed by your instructor.

Done! You have completed Skill Check

Assess Your Skills 1

To complete this project, you will need the following file:

- New blank WordPad document

You will save your files as:

- Lastname_Firstname_ie9_01_Nations
- Lastname_Firstname_ie9_01_Nations_MHT

1. In **Internet Explorer**, navigate to doi.gov to display the U.S. Department of Interior home page. On the navigation bar, point to **What We Do**, and then click **Native American Nations**.

2. Scroll down the page to display the **Economic Development** paragraph, and then click the paragraph's **Learn more** hyperlink. Add the page to your **Favorites** with the name Indian Affairs

3. Click the **Back** button, and then open the **Site Map** in a new tab.

4. Click the first tab—**Native American Nations**. In the **Economic Development** section, select the text *American Recovery and Reinvestment Act of 2009*. Click the **Accelerator** button and then click **Search with Bing**.

5. Add the current tabs to the **Favorites** in a folder named Native American Nations Open the **Organize Favorites** dialog box, and then move the **Indian Affairs** favorite into the **Native American Nations** folder. Display the contents of the **Native American Nations** folder, and then compare your screen with **Figure 1**.

6. Create a **Full-Screen Snip**, click **Copy**, and then **Close** the markup window without saving the changes. **Start** WordPad. Type your first and last name, press [Enter], and then type IE 9 Chapter 2 Assess Your Skills 1

7. Create a new line, and then click **Paste**. Save the document in your **Internet Explorer 9 Chapter 2** folder with the name Lastname_Firstname_ie9_01_Nations

8. If you are printing this project, print the document. **Exit** WordPad.

9. In **Internet Explorer**, delete the **Native American Nations** folder, and then click **Close**.

10. **Close** all but the first tab, and then scroll to the top of the page. Below the page header, click the **Print** hyperlink. Under **Economic Development**, select the first paragraph that begins *Under the American Recovery*. Compare your screen with **Figure 2**.

11. Open the **Print** dialog box and then select the option to print just the selection. If you are printing this project, click **Print**. Otherwise, click **Cancel**. **Close** the printer friendly page.

12. Save the current page as a **Web Archive, single file (*.mht)** file in your **Internet Explorer 9 Chapter 2** folder with the name Lastname_Firstname_ie9_01_Nations_MHT

13. **Close** Internet Explorer. Submit your printouts or files as directed by your instructor.

Done! You have completed Assess Your Skills 1

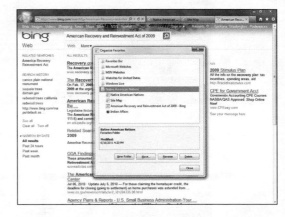

Figure 1

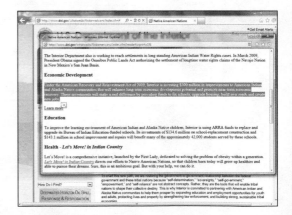

Figure 2

Assess Your Skills 2

To complete this project, you will need the following file:

- New blank WordPad document

You will save your file as:

- Lastname_Firstname_ie9_01_NWR

Figure 1

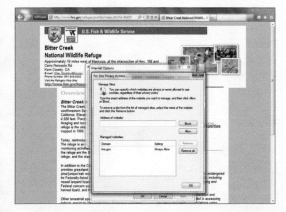

Figure 2

1. Start **Internet Explorer**. Click the **New Tab** button, and then open a new **InPrivate Browsing** window.

2. Search Bing using the terms National Wildlife Refuge In the search results, click the link **National Wildlife Refuge System**. Alternately, navigate to www.fws.gov/refuges

3. Use the **Search the NWRS Site** search box to search the site using the terms Bitter Creek In the search results, click the **Bitter Creek National Wildlife Refuge** hyperlink.

4. Below the text **Overview**, select the text *Bitter Creek National Wildlife Refuge*, and then use the **Map with Bing** Accelerator to open its map. Compare your screen with **Figure 1**.

5. Create a **Full-Screen Snip**, click **Copy**, and then **Close** the markup window without saving the changes. **Start** WordPad. Type your first and last name, press [Enter], and then type IE 9 Chapter 2 Assess Your Skills 2

6. Create a new line, and then click **Paste**. Press [Enter], and then type InPrivate Search Save the file in your **Internet Explorer 9 Chapter 2** file list with the name Lastname_Firstname_ie9_01_NWR

7. In the **InPrivate** window, **Close** the tab with the Bing map, and then display the *fws.gov* **Website privacy policy**. In the **Privacy Report**, click the **Settings** button.

8. In the **Privacy tab** of the **Internet Options** dialog box, click **Sites**, and then set *fws.gov* to **Always Allow**. Compare your screen with **Figure 2**.

9. Create a **Full-Screen Snip**, click **Copy**, and then **Close** the markup window without saving changes. In **WordPad**, create a new line, and then click **Paste**. Press [Enter], and then type Privacy Settings

10. In **Internet Explorer**, remove **fws.gov** from the list of managed websites, and then click **OK**.

11. In the **Internet Options** dialog box, click the **Security tab**, and then display the settings for the **Trusted sites** zone.

12. Create a **Full-Screen Snip**, click **Copy**, and then **Close** the markup window without saving the changes. In **WordPad**, create a new line, and then click **Paste**. Press [Enter], and then type Trusted Sites Zone If you are printing this project, print the WordPad document.

13. **Save**, and then **Exit** WordPad. In the **Internet Options** dialog box, click **Cancel**, and then **Close** the **Privacy Report**.

14. **Close** all Internet Explorer windows. Submit your printout or file as directed by your instructor.

Done! You have completed Assess Your Skills 2

Assess Your Skills Visually

To complete this project, you will need the following file:

- New blank WordPad document

You will save your file as:

- Lastname_Firstname_ie9_01_Agencies

Use the skills you have practiced in this chapter to locate the home pages for the following government agencies: NOAA's National Ocean Service, U.S. Geological Survey, U.S Forest Service, Farm Service Agency, National Register of Historic Places, and the National Center for Education Statistics. Open each home page in its own tab, as shown in **Figure 1**.

Add the tabs as a group to your Favorites in a folder named Agencies Open the **Organize Favorites** dialog box, and then display the **Agencies** folder, as shown in **Figure 1**. Create a **Full-Screen Snip**. **Copy** the snip, and then **Close** the markup window. **Start** WordPad and type your first and last name. Add a new line, and then type IE 9 Chapter 2 Assess Your Skills Visually Add a new line and then **Paste** the snip. **Save** the document in your **Internet Explorer 9 Chapter 2** folder with the name Lastname_ Firstname_ie9_01_Agencies

In your **Favorites**, delete the **Agencies** folder. Print the WordPad document or submit the file as directed by your instructor.

Done! You have completed Assess Your Skills Visually

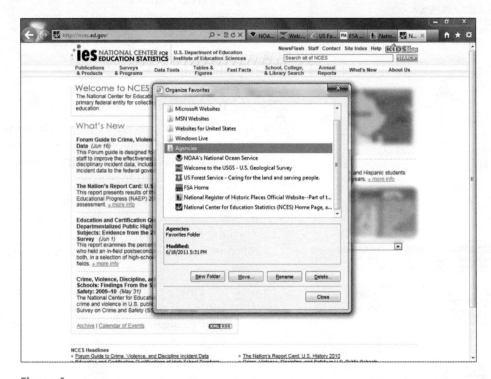

Figure 1

Skills in Context

To complete this project, you will need the following file:

- New blank WordPad document

You will save your file as:

- Lastname_Firstname_ie9_01_Parks

Assume that you are researching national and state parks in California. Use the skills that you have practiced in this chapter to search at least eight websites with information about different California parks. Use your browsing history list to open each page in its own window, and then add the entire group as a favorite in a folder named California Parks

Open the **California Parks** favorite as a group, open the **Organize Favorites** dialog box, and then display the contents of the **California Parks** folder.

Create a **Full-Screen Snip**, and then **Copy** the snip. **Start** WordPad, and type your first and last name. Add a new line, and then type IE 9 Chapter 2 Skills in Context **Paste** the snip on a new line, and then **Save** the document in your **Internet Explorer 9 Chapter 2** folder with the name Lastname_Firstname_ie9_01_ Parks Delete the **California Parks** favorites folder, and then **Exit** Internet Explorer. Submit as directed by your instructor.

Done! You have completed Skills in Context

Skills and You

To complete this project, you will need the following file:

- New blank WordPad document

You will save your file as:

- Lastname_Firstname_ie9_01_Weather

Using the skills that you have practiced in this chapter, use tools on the page at www.nws.noaa.gov to display the weekly weather forecast for your locality. When you are done, create a **Full-screen snip**. Copy the snip, and then paste it into a **WordPad** document

named Lastname_Firstname_ie9_01_Weather In the WordPad document, include your name. Submit as directed by your instructor.

Done! You have completed Skills and You

CHAPTER 3

Getting Started with Windows 7

▶ You use Windows 7 to work with your computer. For example, you start programs, move between windows, and save your work.

▶ In Windows 7, you organize your work by naming files and placing those files into folders that you create.

Your starting screen will look like this:

SKILLS

At the end of this chapter, you will be able to:

Skill 1   Personalize the Windows 7 Desktop

Skill 2   Add and Remove Gadgets

Skill 3   Add Shortcuts

Skill 4   Move Between Windows and Customize the Taskbar

Skill 5   Resize, Move, and Scroll Windows

Skill 6   Use Windows Explorer and Create Folders

Skill 7   Move and Rename Folders and Copy Files

Skill 8   Move, Rename, and Delete Files

Skill 9   Compress Files and Use the Address Bar

Skill 10   Describe and Find Files and Folders

MORE SKILLS

More Skills 11   Create Backup Copies of Your Work

More Skills 12   Use Libraries to Organize Files

More Skills 13   Search the Web with Internet Explorer 8

More Skills 14   View Pictures from Digital Cameras

Outcome

Using the skills listed to the left will enable you to configure your computer similar to these:

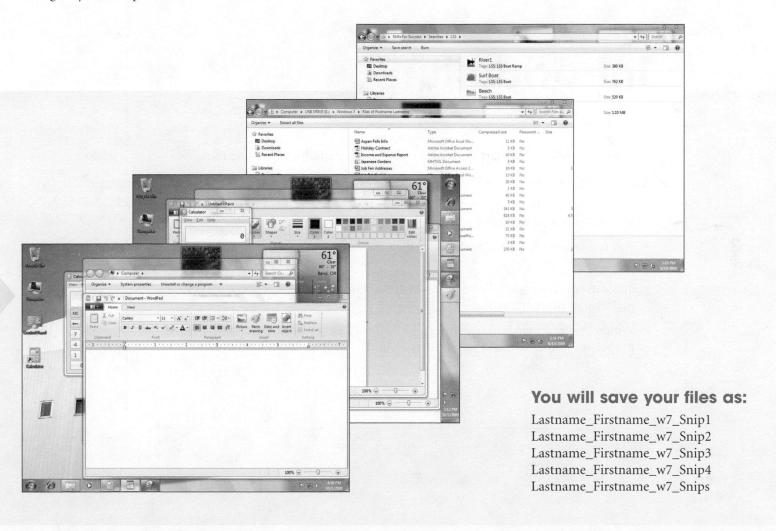

You will save your files as:

Lastname_Firstname_w7_Snip1
Lastname_Firstname_w7_Snip2
Lastname_Firstname_w7_Snip3
Lastname_Firstname_w7_Snip4
Lastname_Firstname_w7_Snips

In this chapter, you will create documents for the Aspen Falls City Hall, which provides essential services for the citizens and visitors of Aspen Falls, California.

Introduction

- ▶ You use Windows 7 to start programs, move between windows, and save files.

- ▶ You can personalize the appearance of Windows 7.

- ▶ You can work with multiple programs and move between them to see the information that you need.

- ▶ You can create and name folders and then move or copy your work into the folders you created.

- ▶ You can combine several files or folders into a single file to save space and to make them more manageable.

- ▶ Windows 7 can help you search for files and folders, and you can assign properties to files to make them easier to find.

Time to complete all 10 skills—
50 to 90 minutes

**Student data files needed
for this chapter:**

■ 01_student_data_files folder

Find your student data files here:

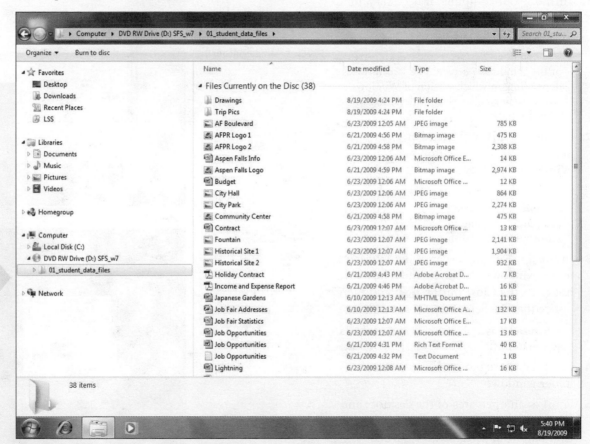

► Windows 7 is an *operating system*—software that controls the hardware in your computer.

► Windows 7 uses a *graphical user interface (GUI)*—an interface that uses graphics or pictures to represent commands and actions.

1. Turn on your computer. If necessary, follow the log on instructions required for the computer you are using.

    The Windows *desktop* is the working area of the Windows 7 screen. The screen varies depending on which version of Windows you are using and how your desktop has been configured.

2. On the left side of the taskbar, *click*—press the left mouse button one time—the **Windows Explorer** button 📁, and then compare your screen with **Figure 1**.

    A *window* is a rectangular box that displays programs, files, and folders. Here, the Libraries window displays.

3. In the upper right corner of the **Libraries** folder window title bar, point to, but do not click, the **Close** button ❌, and then notice that the ScreenTip *Close* displays.

    A *ScreenTip* is a small note that describes a screen element.

4. Click the **Close** button ❌ to close the folder window.

5. Point to an open area of the desktop, and then click the right mouse button. Compare your screen with **Figure 2**.

    A *menu* is a list of commands within a category. *Shortcut menus* list *context-sensitive commands*—actions commonly used when working with the selected object.

■ **Continue to the next page to complete the skill**

Libraries folder window (your window size may be different)

Taskbar

Windows Explorer button

Figure 1

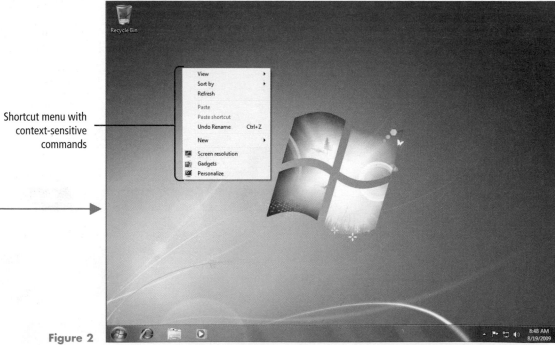

Shortcut menu with context-sensitive commands

Figure 2

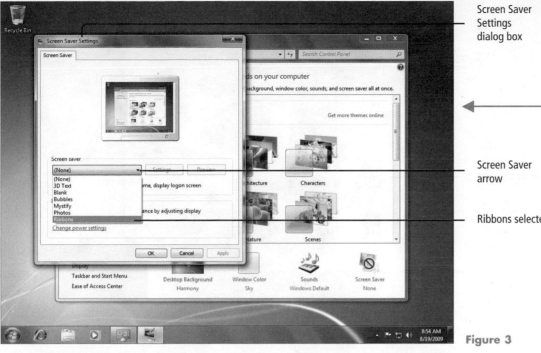

Screen Saver
Settings
dialog box

Screen Saver
arrow

Ribbons selected

Figure 3

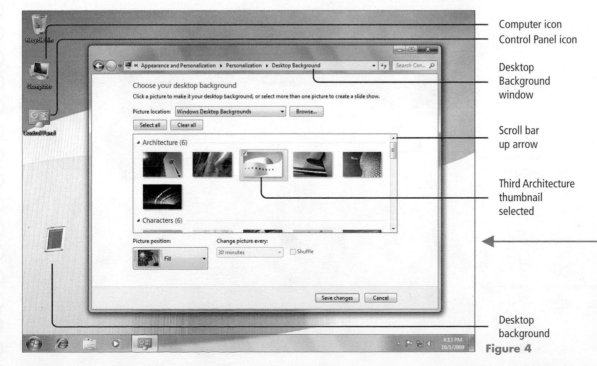

Computer icon
Control Panel icon

Desktop
Background
window

Scroll bar
up arrow

Third Architecture
thumbnail
selected

Desktop
background

Figure 4

6. From the shortcut menu, point to **Personalize**, and then click one time with the left mouse button.

7. In the bottom right corner of the **Personalization** window, click **Screen Saver**.

8. In the **Screen Saver Settings** dialog box, click the **Screen saver arrow**, and from the displayed list, point to **Ribbons**. Compare your screen with **Figure 3**, and then click **Ribbons**.

   A *screen saver* is an animation that displays on your screen after a set period of computer inactivity. A *dialog box* is a box that asks you to make a decision about an individual object or topic.

9. In the **Screen Saver Settings** dialog box, click the **Preview** button to preview a full-screen version of the screen saver. When you are done, move the mouse, and then click **Cancel**.

10. In the left pane of the **Personalization** window, click **Change desktop icons**.

11. At the top of the **Desktop Icon Settings** dialog box, select—click to add a check mark to—the **Computer** and **Control Panel** check boxes. Click **OK** to add the two icons to the left side of the desktop.

12. At the bottom of the **Personalization** window, click **Desktop Background**. At the top of the scroll bar, click the **up arrow** ▲ several times to move to the top of the backgrounds list. Under **Architecture**, click the third thumbnail, and then compare your screen with **Figure 4**.

13. Click the **Save changes** button, and then in the **Personalization** window, click the **Close** button ▰✕▰.

■ **You have completed Skill 1 of 10**

▶ *Gadgets* are dynamic programs that can be moved anywhere on your screen.

▶ The *Start menu* gives you access to all of the programs on your computer.

1. In an open area of the desktop, right-click to display a shortcut menu. From the shortcut menu, click **Gadgets**. Compare your screen with **Figure 1**. ──────

2. In the **Gadgets** gallery, double-click the **Weather** gadget. In the **Gadgets** window, click the **Close** button 🗙 .

3. Point to the **Weather** gadget to display the *gadget control*—a four-button tool set used to modify gadgets. In the gadget control, click the **Larger size** button 🔲 .

4. Click the gadget control **Options** button 🔍 , and then in the **Select current location** box, type Bend, OR

5. Press Enter, and then click **OK** to display the current weather for Bend, Oregon.

6. Right-click the desktop, and then click **Gadgets**. In the **Gadgets** gallery, double-click the **Slide Show** gadget. Double-click to add a second **Slide Show** gadget, and then **Close** 🗙 the Gadgets window.

7. Point to the lower **Slide Show** gadget, and then in the gadget controls, click the **Close** button 🗙 to remove the gadget from the desktop.

8. On the remaining **Slide Show** gadget, point to the **Drag gadget** button ▦ , and then *drag*—move the mouse while holding down the left mouse button and then release at the appropriate time—the gadget near the upper edge of the desktop as shown in **Figure 2**. ──────

■ **Continue to the next page to complete the skill** ▶

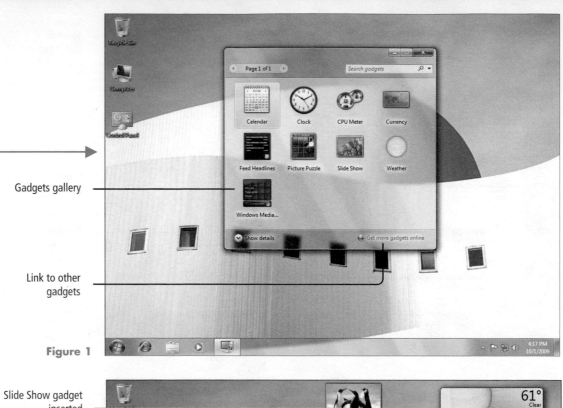

Gadgets gallery

Link to other gadgets

Figure 1

Slide Show gadget inserted and moved

Weather gadget set to large

Current weather in Bend, OR (your weather will be different)

Figure 2

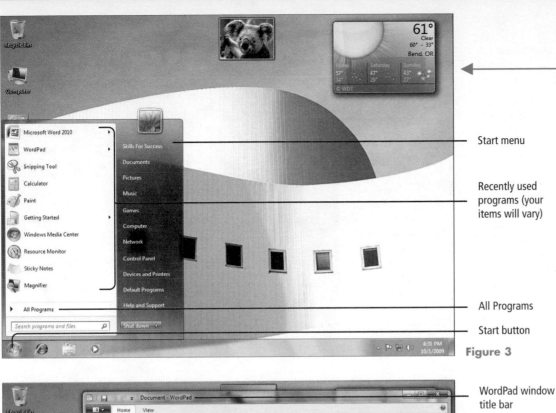

Figure 3

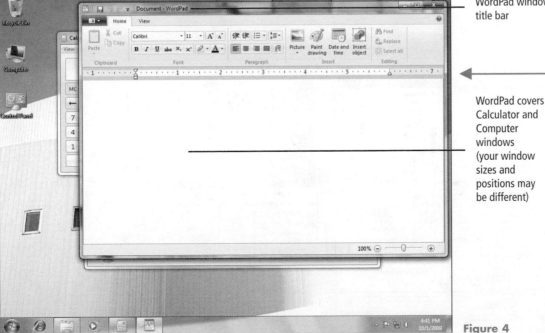

Figure 4

Start menu

Recently used programs (your items will vary)

All Programs

Start button

WordPad window title bar

WordPad covers Calculator and Computer windows (your window sizes and positions may be different)

9. In the lower left corner of the screen, point to and then click the **Start** button, and then compare your screen with **Figure 3**.

The Start menu displays shortcuts to recently used program and common folder windows. The All Programs menu displays the programs installed on your computer.

Your Start menu will display differently than the one in the figure. For example, your list of recently used programs will be different.

10. From the **Start** menu, point to, but do not click, **All Programs** to display a list of programs and program folders. Click the **Accessories** folder, and then from the list, click **Calculator**.

The Calculator program opens, and the Start menu closes. The program's *window name*—*Calculator*—displays in the title bar.

11. Click the **Start** button again. Near the middle of the right side of the **Start** menu, click **Computer**. If the Computer window covers the entire screen, in the upper right corner of the window, click the Restore Down button.

12. Click the **Start** button. In the **Search programs and files** box, type wordpad and then press Enter. If the WordPad window fills the entire screen, click the Restore Down button. Compare your screen with **Figure 4**.

Windows often overlap, but the *active window*—the window in which typing or clicking occurs—displays on top of the other open windows. Here, WordPad is the active window.

■ **You have completed Skill 2 of 10**

► To make a frequently used program quickly available, you can pin a *shortcut*—an icon linked to another file or program that opens the file or program—to the Start menu or taskbar. You can also add shortcuts to the desktop.

1. Point to the **WordPad** window title bar. Click and then drag down and to the right to position the window below the **Computer** window title bar. On the left edge of the screen, be sure the three desktop icons display.

2. Click the **Start** button, point to **All Programs**, click **Accessories**, and then right-click **Calculator**.

3. From the displayed shortcut menu, click **Pin to Start Menu**. At the bottom of the **Start** menu, click the **Back** button, and notice that *Calculator* has been added to the pinned programs area as shown in **Figure 1**.

4. Click the **Start** button, point to **All Programs**, click **Accessories**, right-click **Calculator**, and then point to—but do not click—**Send to**. Notice the available commands on the *Send to* list, as shown in **Figure 2**.

5. From the shortcut menu, click **Desktop** (**create shortcut**), and then click in any open area of the desktop to close the Start menu.

■ **Continue to the next page to complete the skill**

WordPad window moved

Calculator in pinned programs area

Figure 1

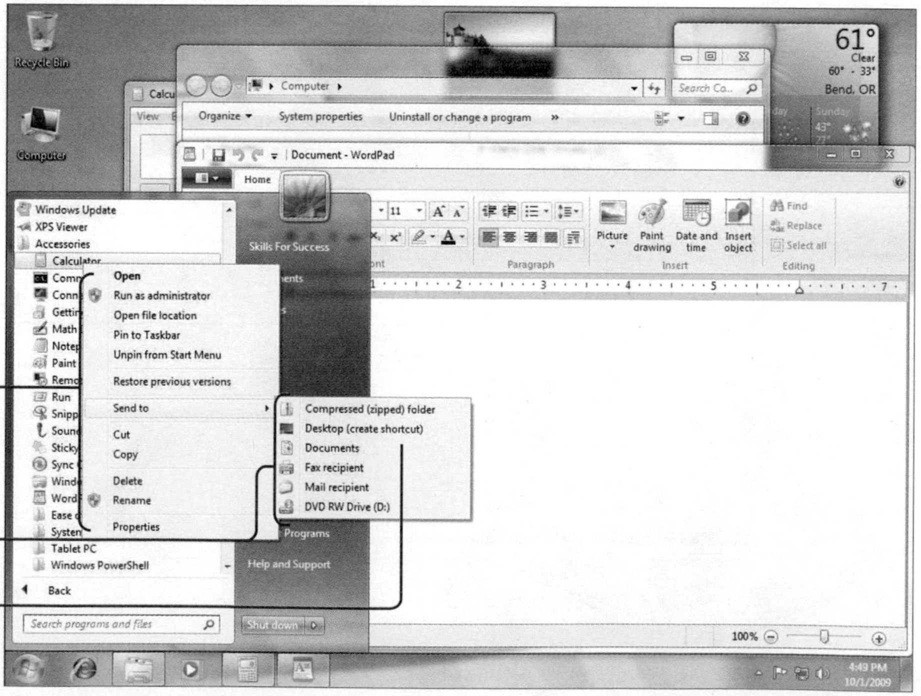

Shortcut menu

Send to submenu

Desktop (create shortcut) command

Figure 2

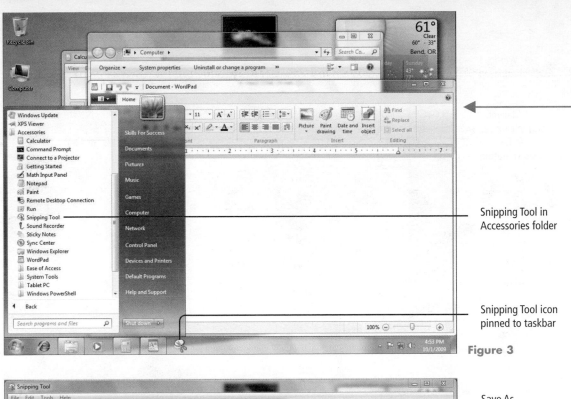

Snipping Tool in
Accessories folder

Snipping Tool icon
pinned to taskbar

Figure 3

6. Click the **Start** button , point to **All Programs**, and then click **Accessories**. In the list of **Accessories** programs, right-click **Snipping Tool**, and then click **Pin to Taskbar**. Compare your screen with **Figure 3**.

> You can use *Snipping Tool* to capture a screen shot, or *snip*, of the entire screen or any object on your screen, and then annotate, save, or share the image. You will use this tool throughout this chapter.

7. Click the **WordPad** window to make it the active window. On the taskbar, click the **Snipping Tool** button .

8. In the **Snipping Tool** window, click the **arrow** to the right of the **New** button—the **New button arrow**—to display a list of snip types. From the list, click **Full-screen Snip**.

9. Near the top of the **Snipping Tool** window, click the **Save Snip** button . In the **Save As** dialog box, under **Favorites**, click **Desktop**. In the **File name** box, using your own last and first name, replace the file name—*Capture*—with Lastname_ Firstname_w7_Snip1 Between words, use the underscore character—hold down [Shift] and then to the right of the 0, press [-].

10. Click the **Save as type** box, and then from the menu, click **JPEG file**. Compare your screen with **Figure 4**, and then click **Save** to save the snip on the desktop.

11. In the upper right corner of the **Snipping Tool** window, click the **Close** button . Notice that your file displays as an icon on the desktop.

■ **You have completed Skill 3 of 10**

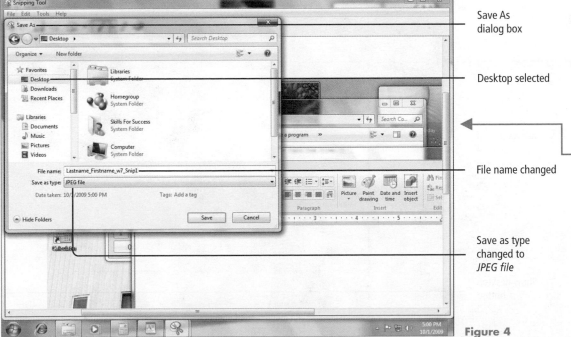

Save As
dialog box

Desktop selected

File name changed

Save as type
changed to
JPEG file

Figure 4

► You can *maximize* a window, which enlarges the window to occupy the entire screen, and you can *restore* a window, which reduces the window to the size it was before being maximized.

► You can also *minimize* a window, which reduces the window to a button on the taskbar, removing it from the desktop without actually closing it.

1. In the **WordPad** window, click the **Maximize** button so that the window covers the entire screen as shown in **Figure 1**.

2. Click the **Restore Down** button to return the window to its former shape, size, and location.

3. In the **WordPad** window, click the **Minimize** button .

4. In the taskbar, click the **Calculator** button to restore the **Calculator** window. Then, click the **WordPad** button to restore the **WordPad** window.

5. Move the pointer to the lower right corner of the taskbar to point to the **Show desktop** button as shown in **Figure 2**.

6. Click the **Show desktop** button to hide all windows. Click the **Show desktop** button again to display all open windows.

7. In the taskbar, click the **Calculator** button to make the Calculator the active window.

8. Point to the **Calculator** title bar, hold down the left mouse button, and then *shake*—move the window back and forth quickly—the window to close all other windows.

■ **Continue to the next page to complete the skill**

WordPad
maximized

Maximize
button changes
to Restore
Down button

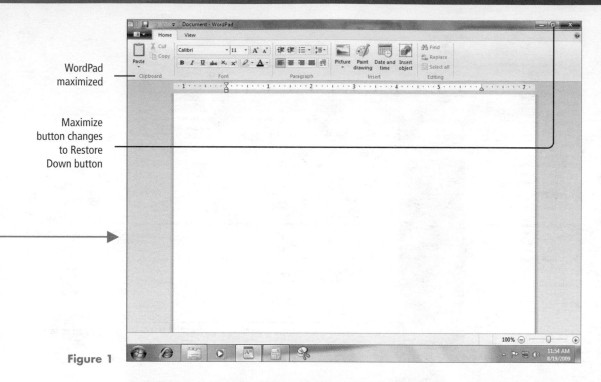

Figure 1

Transparent
windows (only if
Aero feature
is enabled)

Show desktop
button

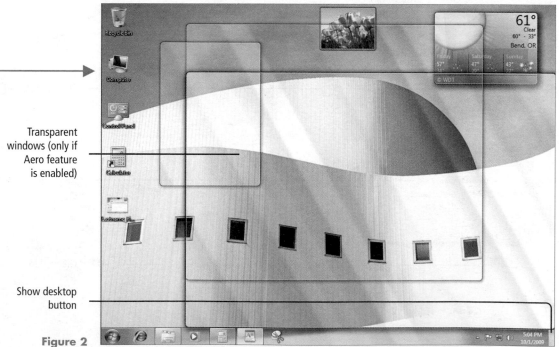

Figure 2

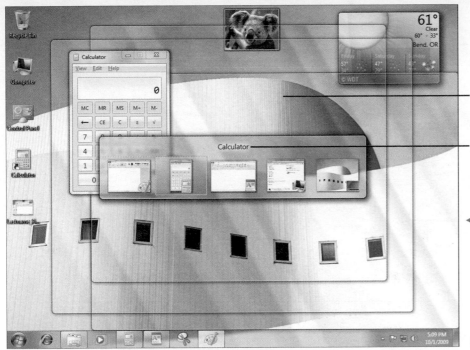

Switching windows with ALT + TAB (with Aero enabled)

Calculator is active window

Figure 3

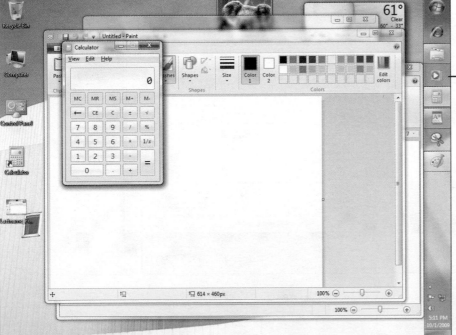

Taskbar displays on right side of screen

Figure 4

9. Shake the **Calculator** window again to display all open windows.

10. Click the **Start** button [icon], point to **All Programs**, click **Accessories**, and then click **Paint**. If the Paint window is maximized, click the Restore Down button [icon].

11. Hold down the [Alt] key, and then press the [Tab] key. Continue to hold down [Alt], and press [Tab] several times. Notice that the selected window moves from left to right in the list of thumbnails. Move to the **Calculator** window as shown in **Figure 3**, and then release [Alt].

12. On the taskbar, point to the **Computer** icon and right-click to display a *jump list*—a list of related files or commands that you might want to jump to.

13. Right-click an open area of the taskbar, and then from the shortcut menu, click **Properties**. In the **Taskbar and Start Menu Properties** dialog box, click the **Taskbar location on screen arrow**, and then click **Right**. Click **OK** and compare your screen with **Figure 4**.

14. In the taskbar, click the **Snipping Tool** button [icon]. In the **Snipping Tool** window, click the **New button arrow**, and then click **Full-screen Snip**. Click the **Save Snip** button [icon], and then in the **Save As** dialog box, click **Desktop**. In the **File name** box, type Lastname_Firstname_w7_Snip2 With **JPEG file** selected, click **Save**, and then **Close** [icon] the Snipping Tool.

15. Use the technique you practiced to return the taskbar to the bottom of the desktop.

■ **You have completed Skill 4 of 10**

► You can move, resize, and scroll windows to view the information you need.

1. On the right side of the taskbar, click the **Show desktop** button ▌ to hide all of the windows.

2. On the taskbar, click the **Windows Explorer** button. Move the pointer to the lower right corner of the **Computer** window to display the 🔲 pointer as shown in **Figure 1**.

3. Drag diagonally up and to the left until you see scroll bars, and then release the mouse button. Adjust as necessary so that the **Computer** window is the approximate size of the one shown in **Figure 2**.

   A *scroll bar* is added to the window whenever the window contains more content than it can display. Here, two scroll bars display. In a scroll bar, the *scroll box* provides a visual indication of your location in the window. The size of the scroll box varies to indicate the relative size of the information.

4. In the **Computer** window **Navigation** pane, at the bottom of the vertical scroll bar, click the **down arrow** ▾ two times to scroll down.

5. On the same scroll bar, click the **up arrow** ▴ and hold down the left mouse button to scroll to the top.

6. Point to the scroll box, and then drag it downward.

7. At the top of the **Computer** window, point to a blank area in the title bar. Drag the window to the top edge of the desktop, and then release the mouse button to maximize the window.

■ **Continue to the next page to complete the skill** ➤

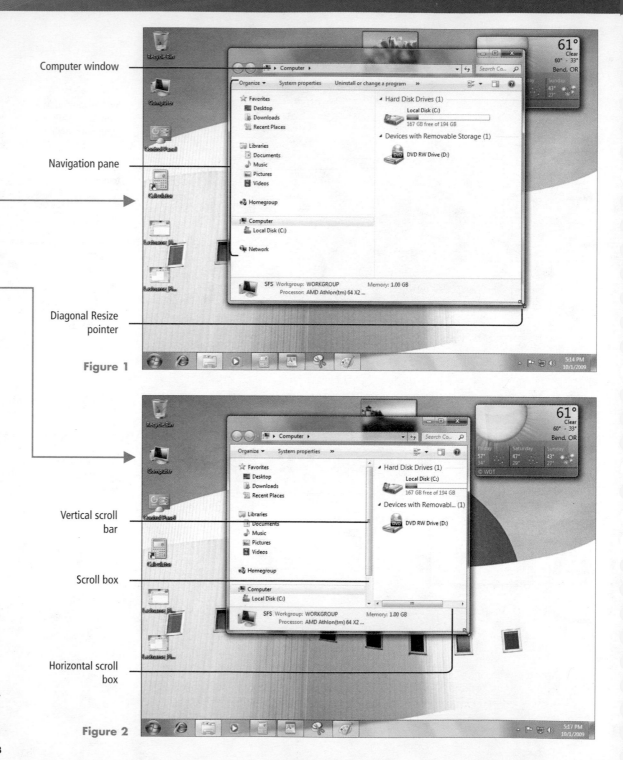

Computer window

Navigation pane

Diagonal Resize pointer

Figure 1

Vertical scroll bar

Scroll box

Horizontal scroll box

Figure 2

WordPad window
snapped to edge
of desktop

Figure 3

Your own name

Snip1 inserted

Snip2 inserted

Figure 4

8. Drag the title bar down to restore the window to its original size, but not its original location.

9. In the **Computer** window, click the **Close** button. In the taskbar, right-click the **Paint** button, and then click **Close window**. Use the same technique to close the **Calculator** window.

10. In the taskbar, click the **WordPad** button to make it the active window. Drag the WordPad window title bar to the right edge of the desktop to snap the WordPad window as shown in **Figure 3**.

11. In the **WordPad** window, type your first and last name, and then press Enter. On the desktop, click the **Lastname_Firstname_ w7_Snip1** icon to display its full name. Drag the icon to the line below your name in the WordPad document, and then release the mouse button.

    A copy of the snip is inserted into the WordPad document.

12. Drag the **Lastname_Firstname_w7_Snip2** file to the line below the figure you previously inserted into the WordPad document. Scroll to the top of the **WordPad** window, and then compare your screen with **Figure 4**.

13. In the top, left corner of the **WordPad** title bar, click the **Save** button. In the **Save As** dialog box, in the **Navigation** pane, click **Desktop**. In the **File name** box, type Lastname_Firstname_w7_Snips and then click **Save**.

14. **Close** the WordPad window.

■ **You have completed Skill 5 of 10**

► *Windows Explorer* is a program used to create and manage folders, and to copy, move, sort, and delete files.

► When you have a new category of files to store, you can create a new folder.

1. On the taskbar, click the **Windows Explorer** button 🗖.

2. If the window is not maximized, drag the title bar to the top of the screen. Alternately, on the right side of the title bar, click the Maximize button 🖃.

3. On the toolbar, click the **Organize** button, and then point to **Layout**. If Details pane is not checked, click to select it.

4. In the **Navigation** pane on the left side of the **Computer** window, click **Computer**. Compare your screen with **Figure 1**. If necessary, to the left of Computer, click the open arrow ▷.

   The open arrow changes to a filled arrow pointing downward ◢.

5. Insert your USB flash drive or another removable drive. If the AutoPlay dialog box displays, click Close 🗙. In the Navigation pane, under Computer, click your removable drive. Compare your screen with **Figure 2**.

   For this chapter, the file list is empty; your storage device or drive may already contain files and folders and may be named differently.

Open/close arrow

File list

Details pane

Figure 1

■ **Continue to the next page to complete the skill** ▶

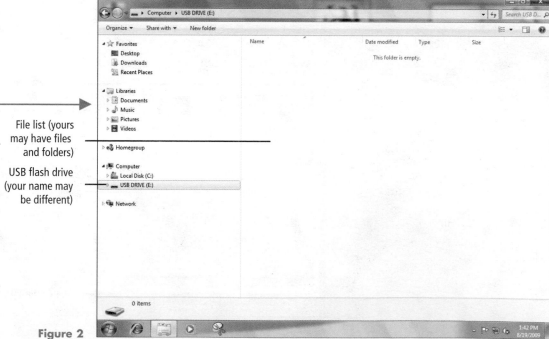

File list (yours may have files and folders)

USB flash drive (your name may be different)

Figure 2

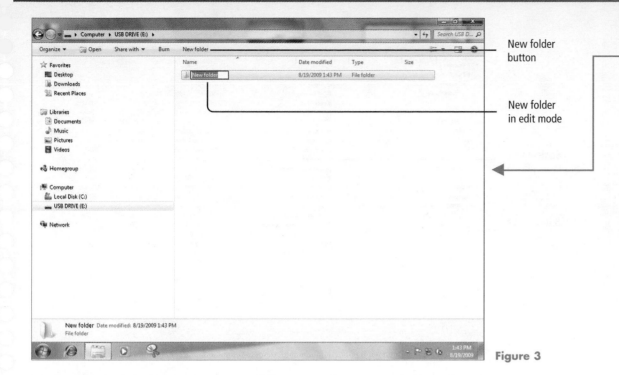

New folder
button

New folder
in edit mode

Figure 3

Windows 7 folder

Resize pointer

Name column
heading

Figure 4

6. With the flash drive selected, in the tool-bar, click the **New folder** button. Compare your screen with **Figure 3**.

   A new folder—named *New folder*—is cre-ated with the name of the folder displayed in ***edit mode***—a mode in which you can change the name of a file or folder.

7. With *New folder* in edit mode, type Windows 7 and then press Enter. Double-click the **Windows 7** folder to display its file list.

8. Right-click the file list, point to **New**, and then click **Folder**. Substitute your name where indicated, type Pictures of Firstname Lastname and then press Enter.

9. Use either technique just practiced to cre-ate a new folder named Documents of Firstname Lastname

10. In the file list, click the **Name** column heading as many times as needed to sort the content from *a* to *z* and then from *z* to *a*.

    The arrow in the Name column heading points up when the folders are displayed in ***ascending order*** (*a* to *z*) and points down when the folders are displayed in ***descending order*** (*z* to *a*).

11. Click as needed to sort the folders in descending alphabetical order—from *z* to *a*.

12. In the file list, move the pointer to the left of the **Date modified** column heading to display the resize pointer ⊕, as shown in **Figure 4**.

13. Drag the resize pointer ⊕ to the right to make the **Name** column slightly wider than the longest folder name. Alternately, double-click.

■ **You have completed Skill 6 of 10**

▶ You can move the folders, including the files in the folders, from another location to your flash drive or other storage device.

1. Navigate to the location where your student files for this book are stored. They may be stored on a CD, in a course management system, on a hard drive, or on a shared network drive. In this chapter, the data CD is used.

2. In the **Navigation** pane, click the **CD open arrow** ▷, and then click the **01_student_data_files** folder.

3. In the **Navigation** pane, if necessary, click the **open arrow** ▷ to the left of your storage device as shown in **Figure 1**.

4. Near the top of the file list, drag the **Drawings** folder to the **Navigation** pane directly on top of your **Windows 7** folder. When the ScreenTip says *Copy to Windows 7*, release the mouse button.

5. Repeat the procedure just practiced to copy the **Trip Pics** folder to your **Windows 7** folder.

6. In the **Navigation** pane, click your **Windows 7** folder. In the file list, right-click the **Drawings** folder, click **Rename**, type Drawings of Firstname Lastname and then press Enter. Compare your screen with **Figure 2**.

7. In the **Navigation** pane, under **Computer**, locate and click the folder named **01_student_data_files** to display its file list.

8. Near the middle of the file list, drag the **City Hall** file to your **Windows 7** folder.

■ **Continue to the next page to complete the skill**

Student files display in file list

USB flash drive opened

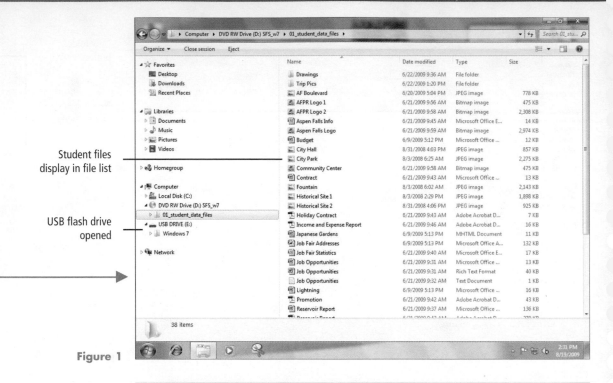

Figure 1

Trip Pics folder copied

Folder copied and renamed

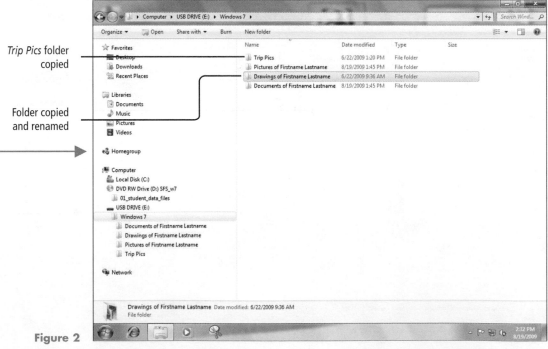

Figure 2

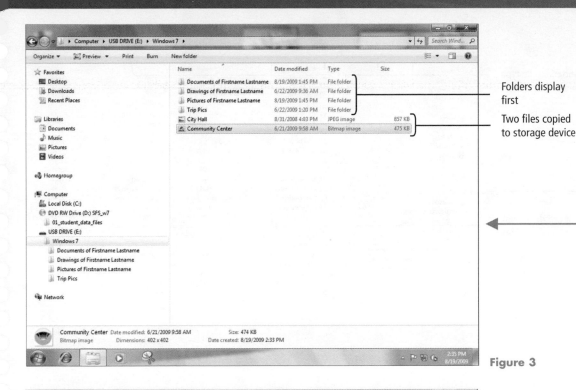

Folders display first

Two files copied to storage device

Figure 3

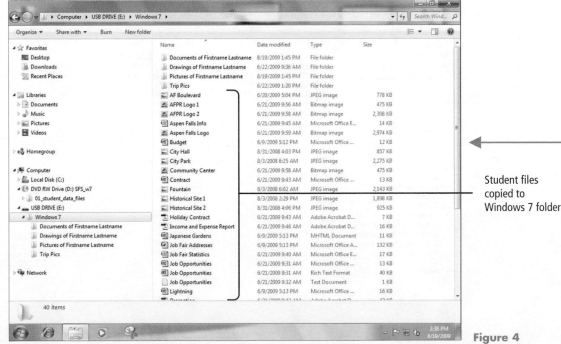

Student files copied to Windows 7 folder

Figure 4

9. Right-click the **Community Center** file, and then from the shortcut menu, click **Copy**.

   This creates a copy of the *Community Center* file and places it in a temporary storage area called the *Clipboard*.

10. In the **Navigation** pane, click your **Windows 7** folder. Right-click an open area of the file list, and then click **Paste** to copy the file.

11. Sort the **Name** column in ascending order and compare your screen with **Figure 3**.

    In a file list, the folders and files are sorted into two separate lists. Here, folders are listed first.

12. Display the **01_student_data_files** file list again. Click the **AFPR Logo 1** file, hold down Shift, and then click the **Aspen Falls Logo** file to select all the files between the first and last files. Drag one of the selected files to your **Windows 7** folder to copy all four files.

13. Click the **AF Boulevard** file, hold down Ctrl, click the **Budget** file, and then click the **City Park** file. With the three files selected, drag one of the files to your **Windows 7** folder.

14. In the file list, click the **Contract** file. Scroll to the bottom of the file list. Hold down Shift, and then click the **Zoning Report** file. Drag the selected files to your **Windows 7** folder. Display your **Windows 7** file list, and then compare your screen with **Figure 4**.

■ **You have completed Skill 7 of 10**

▶ When you drag a file or folder to another place on the same drive, the file or folder is moved—not copied—to that location.

▶ You can rename or delete files when you no longer need them.

1. If necessary, display your **Windows 7** file list.

2. In the file list, click the **Type** column header to sort the files by file type. Point to the right border of the **Type** column heading, and then with the ⊞ pointer, double-click to resize the column.

3. In the file list, use the wheel in the middle of your mouse or the vertical scroll bar to scroll down until you can see all of the **Microsoft Office Word Document** files. If necessary, in the Navigation pane, click your Windows 7 folder open arrow ▷ to display its folders, and scroll as needed to display all four folders as shown in **Figure 1**.

4. Click the **Budget** file, hold down Shift, and then click the **Survey Letter** file to select all the Word documents. Drag the selected files to the **Documents of Firstname Lastname** folder to move them to the folder.

5. In the **Navigation** pane, click the **Documents of Firstname Lastname** folder to display the moved files as shown in **Figure 2**.

Sorted by file type

Word document files

Windows 7 folders

Word documents moved to folder

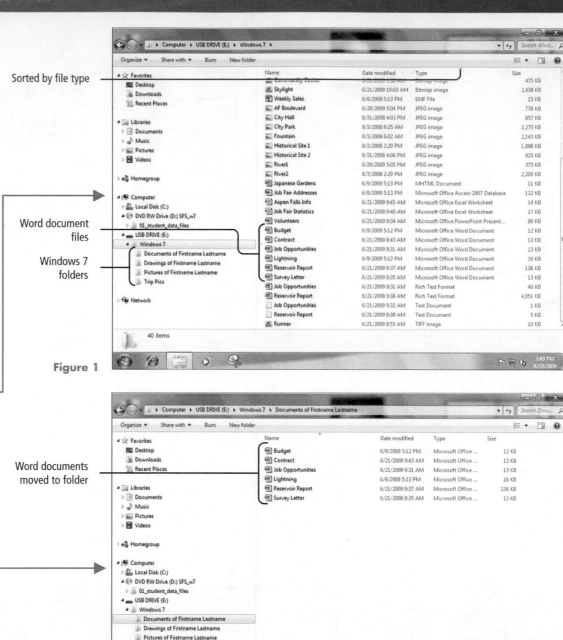

Figure 1

Figure 2

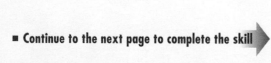

■ **Continue to the next page to complete the skill**

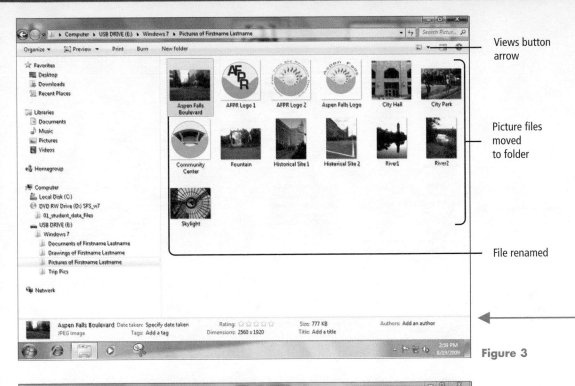

Views button arrow

Picture files moved to folder

File renamed

Figure 3

6. In the **Navigation** pane, click your **Windows 7** folder. Use the technique just practiced to move the eight **JPEG image** files to the **Pictures of Firstname Lastname** folder.

7. Move the five Bitmap images—**BMP File**—to the **Pictures of Firstname Lastname** folder.

8. In the **Navigation** pane, click the **Pictures of Firstname Lastname** folder. On the toolbar, click the **Views button arrow** [icon], and then if it is not already selected, click **Large Icons**.

9. In the file list, right-click the **AF Boulevard** file, and then click **Rename**. Type Aspen Falls Boulevard and then press [Enter]. Compare your screen with **Figure 3**.

10. In the file list, right-click the **Historical Site 2** file, and then click **Delete**. The **Delete File** message box displays, as shown in **Figure 4**.

> When you delete files from removable storage such as a USB flash drive, the files are typically deleted permanently.

11. In the **Delete File** message box, click **Yes**.

12. In the upper left corner of the window, click the **Back** button [icon] to move back to your Windows 7 folder. Alternately, in the Navigation pane, click your Windows 7 folder.

13. In the file list, right-click the **Trip Pics** folder, and then click **Delete**. In the displayed **Delete Folder** message box, click **Yes**.

> When you delete a folder, all files in the folder are also deleted.

■ **You have completed Skill 8 of 10**

Permanently delete file message

Figure 4

▶ You can *compress*—reduce the file size of—one or more files into a single file. Compression is often used to combine many files into one file for easy distribution.

▶ You can use the address bar at the top of the Windows Explorer window to move to a desired location.

1. With your **Windows 7** file list displayed, sort the **Name** column in ascending order.

2. Click the **Aspen Falls Info** file, hold down Shift, and then click the **Zoning Report** file. If necessary, in the Details pane, click Show more details, and then notice that the 17 files have a total size of about 5 MB as shown in **Figure 1**.

3. In the file list, right-click one of the selected files, and then from the displayed shortcut menu, point to **Send to**. Click **Compressed (zipped) folder**, and then wait a moment for the files to be compressed.

   The compressed folder displays the name of the file that you right-clicked, and it is in edit mode so you can change the file name.

4. With the compressed file in edit mode, type Files of Firstname Lastname and then press Enter. Sort by file name and click **Files of Firstname Lastname** to display its details as shown in **Figure 2**.

   The compressed folder is about 1.6 MB—which is about 68% smaller than the original file.

■ **Continue to the next page to complete the skill** ➤

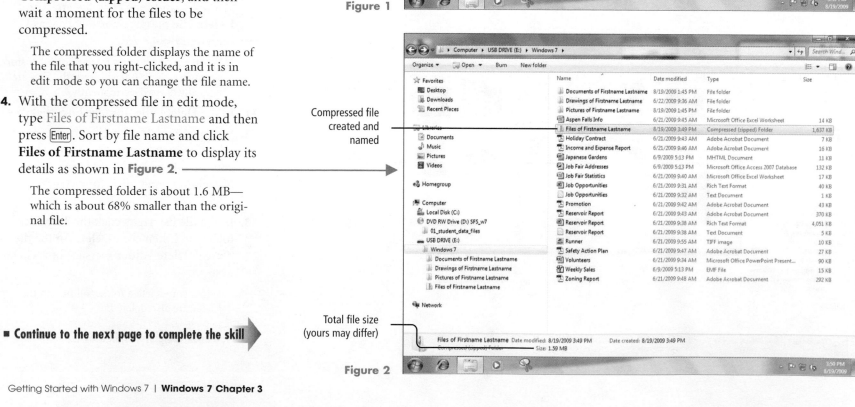

File size of selected files

Figure 1

Compressed file created and named

Total file size (yours may differ)

Figure 2

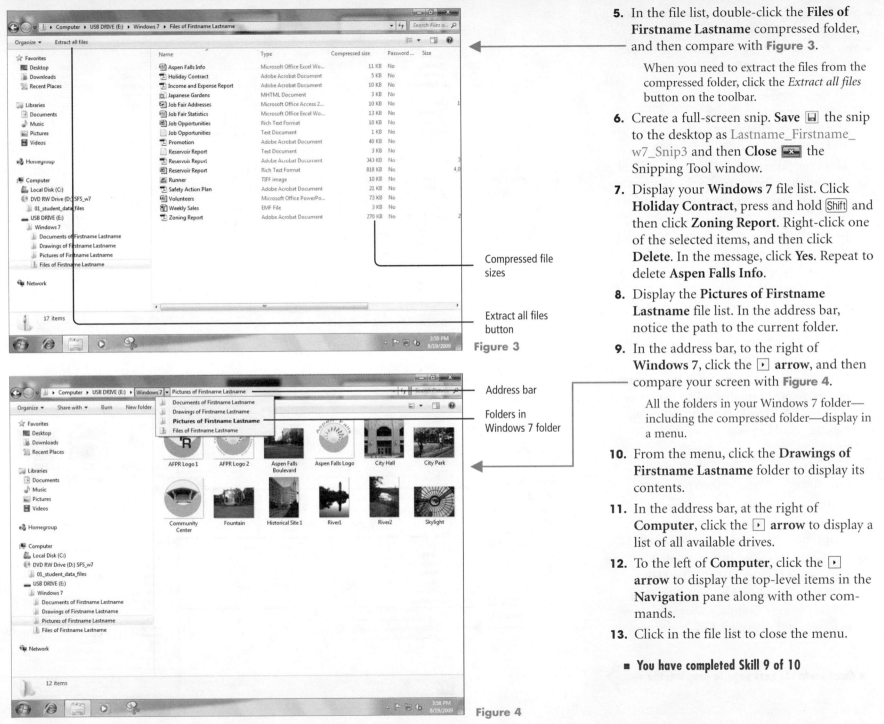

Compressed file sizes

Extract all files button

Figure 3

Address bar

Folders in Windows 7 folder

Figure 4

5. In the file list, double-click the **Files of Firstname Lastname** compressed folder, and then compare with **Figure 3**.

   When you need to extract the files from the compressed folder, click the *Extract all files* button on the toolbar.

6. Create a full-screen snip. **Save** 🔲 the snip to the desktop as Lastname_Firstname_ w7_Snip3 and then **Close** ▣ the Snipping Tool window.

7. Display your **Windows 7** file list. Click **Holiday Contract**, press and hold Shift and then click **Zoning Report**. Right-click one of the selected items, and then click **Delete**. In the message, click **Yes**. Repeat to delete **Aspen Falls Info**.

8. Display the **Pictures of Firstname Lastname** file list. In the address bar, notice the path to the current folder.

9. In the address bar, to the right of **Windows 7**, click the ▶ arrow, and then compare your screen with **Figure 4**.

   All the folders in your Windows 7 folder— including the compressed folder—display in a menu.

10. From the menu, click the **Drawings of Firstname Lastname** folder to display its contents.

11. In the address bar, at the right of **Computer**, click the ▶ arrow to display a list of all available drives.

12. To the left of **Computer**, click the ▶ arrow to display the top-level items in the **Navigation** pane along with other commands.

13. Click in the file list to close the menu.

■ **You have completed Skill 9 of 10**

▶ Windows 7 has several search methods you can use to find files and folders.

▶ You can also add *tags*—custom file properties that help you find and organize your files.

1. From your storage device, display the **Drawings of Firstname Lastname** file list, and then click the first file—**Beach**.

2. Move the pointer to the line at the top of the **Details** pane to display the 🔲 pointer, and then drag to display three lines of details.

3. In the **Details** pane, in the **Tags** box, click the text **Add a tag**. Type LSS and then press ➡. Type LSS Boat and then compare your screen with **Figure 1**.

4. Press Enter to confirm the tags. Use the procedure just practiced—type, do not use the check boxes—to add the same two tags to the **Surf Boat** file.

5. In the **Navigation** pane, click the **Pictures of Firstname Lastname** folder, and then click the file **River1**. Type the following tags: LSS and LSS Boat Ramp and then press Enter.

6. In the **Details** pane, click the **Title** box, type River Station and then press Enter.

7. In the file list, right-click the **River1** file, and then click **Properties**. In the **Properties** dialog box, click the **Details** tab.

8. Under **Description**, click the fourth **Rating** star from the left. Under **Origin**, click the **Copyright** box, and then type Public Domain Compare your screen with **Figure 2**, and then click **OK**.

■ **Continue to the next page to complete the skill**

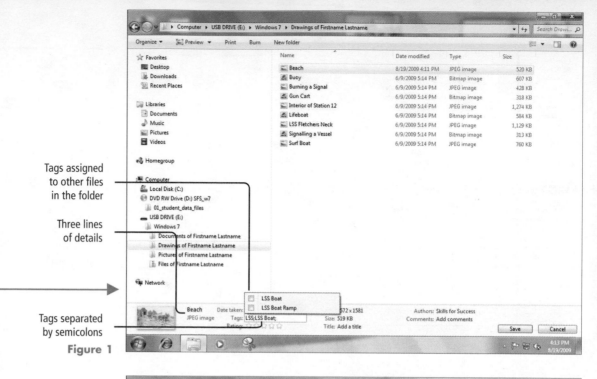

Tags assigned to other files in the folder

Three lines of details

Tags separated by semicolons

Figure 1

Properties dialog box Details tab

Description properties

Copyright property

Figure 2

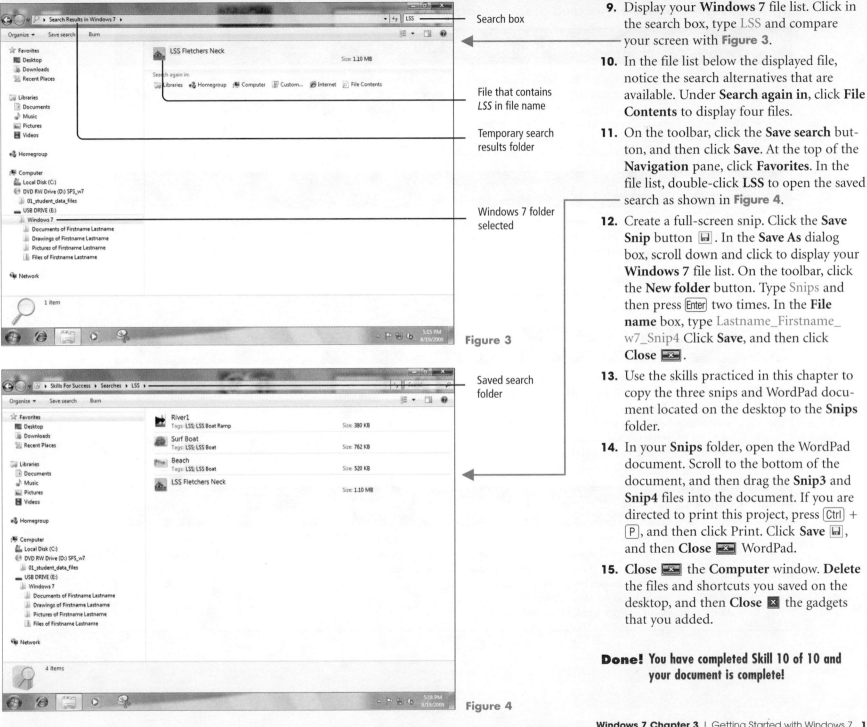

Search box

File that contains *LSS* in file name

Temporary search results folder

Windows 7 folder selected

Figure 3

Saved search folder

Figure 4

9. Display your **Windows 7** file list. Click in the search box, type LSS and compare your screen with **Figure 3**.

10. In the file list below the displayed file, notice the search alternatives that are available. Under **Search again in**, click **File Contents** to display four files.

11. On the toolbar, click the **Save search** button, and then click **Save**. At the top of the **Navigation** pane, click **Favorites**. In the file list, double-click **LSS** to open the saved search as shown in **Figure 4**.

12. Create a full-screen snip. Click the **Save Snip** button 🖫. In the **Save As** dialog box, scroll down and click to display your **Windows 7** file list. On the toolbar, click the **New folder** button. Type Snips and then press ⌗Enter⌗ two times. In the **File name** box, type Lastname_Firstname_w7_Snip4 Click **Save**, and then click **Close** ⌗✕⌗.

13. Use the skills practiced in this chapter to copy the three snips and WordPad document located on the desktop to the **Snips** folder.

14. In your **Snips** folder, open the WordPad document. Scroll to the bottom of the document, and then drag the **Snip3** and **Snip4** files into the document. If you are directed to print this project, press ⌗Ctrl⌗ + ⌗P⌗, and then click Print. Click **Save** 🖫, and then **Close** ⌗✕⌗ WordPad.

15. **Close** ⌗✕⌗ the **Computer** window. **Delete** the files and shortcuts you saved on the desktop, and then **Close** ⌗✕⌗ the gadgets that you added.

Done! You have completed Skill 10 of 10 and your document is complete!

The following More Skills are located at **www.pearsonhighered.com/skills**

More Skills Create Backup Copies of Your Work

When your work relies on computer files, it is a good practice to create copies of your files. In that way, if an active file is lost or damaged, you can work with the copy.

In More Skills 11, you will create a compressed zip file from your Windows 7 folder and then copy it to another computer

drive. To begin, open your Internet browser, navigate to www.pearsonhighered.com/skills, locate the name of your textbook, and follow the instructions on the website.

More Skills Use Libraries to Organize Files

You can organize files and folders stored at various locations on your computer into a library that can be viewed as a collection. You can add folders to existing libraries or add folders to libraries that you create.

In More Skills 12, you will add a folder to an existing library, create your own library, and then add a folder to the new library.

To begin, open your Internet browser, navigate to www.pearsonhighered.com/skills, locate the name of your textbook, and follow the instructions on the website.

More Skills Search the Web with Internet Explorer 8

You can search for information on the Web using several search features in the Internet Explorer 8 Web browser. Some websites that search the Internet—Bing, for example—show a preview of potential websites that meet your search criteria.

In More Skills 13, you will use Internet Explorer 8 to search the Web for information using several websites including

bing.com. To begin, open your Internet browser, navigate to www.pearsonhighered.com/skills, locate the name of your textbook, and follow the instructions on the website.

More Skills View Pictures from Digital Cameras

You can use Windows Photo Viewer to view, print, rotate, copy, and email photos created by a digital camera. You can also change folder window view settings to preview each digital photo and display details about how and when the photo was taken.

In More Skills 14, you will use Windows Photo Viewer to view several digital photos in a folder window. To begin, open

your Internet browser, navigate to www.pearsonhighered.com/skills, locate the name of your textbook, and follow the instructions on the website.

Key Terms

Online Help Skills

1. **Start** your Web browser, for example Internet Explorer. In the Address Bar, type www.microsoft.com/windows/windows-7/features/videos.aspx and then press `Enter` to display the **What's new in Windows 7: Videos Web** page.

2. Turn on your speakers or put on headphones. Scroll down to the **Windows Live** videos, and then click the **SkyDrive** link. The demo will begin as shown in **Figure 1** and is only 1:36 minutes in length. If the video does not play, you might need to install Microsoft Silverlight from www.silverlight.net.

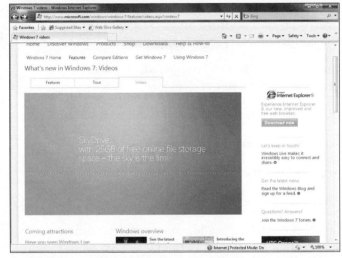

Figure 1

3. Listen to and watch the demonstration, and then see if you can answer the following question: What would you need to do in order to use SkyDrive to access your school work from both home and school?

Matching

Match each term in the second column with its correct definition in the first column by writing the letter of the term on the blank line in front of the correct definition.

____ **1.** Software that controls the hardware attached to your computer.

____ **2.** An interface that uses graphics or pictures to represent commands and actions.

____ **3.** The working area of the Windows 7 screen.

____ **4.** A graphic representation—often a small image on a button—that enables you to run a program or a program function.

____ **5.** A small note, usually displayed in a yellow box, which provides information about or describes a screen element.

____ **6.** A dynamic program that can be moved anywhere on your screen.

____ **7.** A program that captures a screen or part of a screen.

____ **8.** To remove the window from the screen without closing it.

____ **9.** To increase the size of a window to fill the screen.

____ **10.** A program that enables you to create and manage folders, and to copy, move, sort, and delete files.

A Desktop

B Gadget

C Graphical User Interface

D Icon

E Maximize

F Minimize

G Operating System

H ScreenTip

I Snipping Tool

J Windows Explorer

Multiple Choice

Choose the correct answer.

1. GUI is an acronym for _____.
   A. General universal information
   B. Globally unique identifier
   C. Graphical user interface

2. You can activate a shortcut menu by placing the pointer over an object and clicking the _____ mouse button.
   A. Left
   B. Middle
   C. Right

3. A box that asks you to make a decision about an individual object or topic is called a _____ box.
   A. Dialog
   B. Question
   C. Text

4. The button on the left side of the taskbar that is used to open programs, change system settings, find Windows help, or shut down the computer is called the _____ button.
   A. Go
   B. Start
   C. Windows

5. The files and folders stored in the selected disk drive or folder are displayed in the _____ list.
   A. Content
   B. File
   C. Navigation

6. When you create a new folder, the folder name displays in _____ mode.
   A. Copy
   B. Delete
   C. Edit

7. When you copy an item, it is stored in the _____, a temporary storage area in Windows.
   A. Bit locker
   B. CGI bin
   C. Clipboard

8. You can _____ a file or files to reduce the size of the files or combine files to make them easier to send.
   A. Compress
   B. Copy
   C. Merge

9. When you create a search folder, the search name displays in the Navigation pane in the _____ category.
   A. Favorites
   B. Found
   C. Recent Searches

10. A custom file property that is read during searches is the _____ property.
    A. Locate
    B. Statistics
    C. Tags

Topics for Discussion

1. Recall that you can create folders when you have new categories of files to store. Consider what files you currently have and will have on your computer or storage device. What folders do you need to organize these files, and what names would you assign to each folder?

2. Recall that you can pin shortcuts to commonly used programs to the Start menu and taskbar. What programs do you think you would pin to the Start menu or taskbar?

Skill Check

To complete this project, you will need the following file:

- New, blank WordPad document

You will save your files as:

- Lastname_Firstname_w7_SC
- Lastname_Firstname_w7_SC1
- Lastname_Firstname_w7_SC2
- Lastname_Firstname_w7_SC_Zip

1. Turn on your computer, and if necessary, follow the log on instructions required for the computer you are using.

2. Right-click a blank area of the desktop. In the shortcut menu, move the pointer to the bottom of the list, and then click **Personalize**.

3. At the bottom of the **Personalization** window, click the **Desktop Background** button. Use the vertical scroll bar to display the **Architecture** desktop backgrounds, and then click the first thumbnail. Click **Save changes** to apply the new background, and then **Close** the Personalization window.

Figure 1

4. Right-click a blank area of the desktop, and then click **Gadgets**. Double-click the **Slide Show** gadget, and then **Close** the Gadgets window. Point to the **Slide Show** gadget, and then click the **Larger size** button. Drag the gadget to the right of the **Recycle Bin** icon.

5. Click the **Start** button, point to **All Programs**, and then click **Accessories**. Right-click **WordPad**, point to **Send to**, click **Desktop (create shortcut)**, and then click in any open area of the desktop.

6. On the desktop, double-click the **WordPad** icon to start the program. If necessary, snap the **WordPad** window on the right side of the desktop as shown in **Figure 1**.

7. In the **WordPad** window, type your first and last name and then press Enter. Click the **Save** button, and then in the displayed **Save As** dialog box, in the **Navigation** pane, click **Desktop**. In the **File name** box, type Lastname_Firstname_w7_SC and then click **Save**.

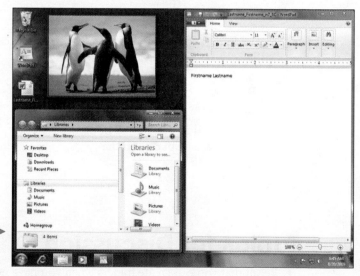

Figure 2

8. If necessary, insert your USB flash drive. On the taskbar, click the **Windows Explorer** button. If necessary, click the Restore Down button. With the ⊠ pointer, resize the **Libraries** folder window approximately as shown in **Figure 2**, and then drag the window's title bar to position the window as shown.

- Continue to the next page to complete this Skill Check ▸

9. In the **Navigation** pane, under **Computer**, display the contents of your storage device. Click the **New folder** button, type Skill Check and then press Enter.

10. If necessary, pin the Snipping Tool to the taskbar. On the taskbar, click the **Snipping Tool** button. In the **Snipping Tool** window, click the **New button arrow**, and then click **Full-screen Snip**.

11. In the **Snipping Tool** window, click the **Save Snip** button. In the **Save As** dialog box, scroll down to display the **Computer** drives. Click your flash drive **arrow** to display its folders, and display your **Skill Check** file list. In the **File name** box, type Lastname_Firstname_w7_SC1 Be sure the **Save as type** box displays **JPEG file**, click **Save**, and then close the **Snipping Tool** window.

12. **Maximize** the folder window, and then display the **Skill Check** file list.

13. Click the snip—**JPEG image**—file to select it. In the **Details** pane, click the **Tags** box, type desktop and then press Enter.

14. In the upper right corner of the window, click in the search box, type desktop and then press Enter. In the displayed **Search Results** folder, click **File Contents** and then compare your screen with **Figure 3**.

Figure 3

15. Create a full-screen snip, **Save** it in your **Skill Check** folder as Lastname_Firstname_w7_SC2 and then close the Snipping Tool window.

16. In the upper right corner of the folder window, click the **Restore Down** button, and then display your **Skill Check** file list.

17. Click the first snip file, press and hold Shift, and then click the second snip file. Drag one of the selected files to a blank area below your name in the **WordPad** window. If you are printing your work, print the WordPad document.

18. In the **WordPad** window, click the **Save** button, and **Close** WordPad.

19. On the desktop, point to the **Lastname_Firstname_w7_SC** file, and then drag the file to a blank area in the **Skill Check** file list to copy the file.

20. **Maximize** the folder window. Sort the files in ascending order, and then select all three files. Right-click the first file, point to **Send to**, and then click **Compressed (zipped) folder**. Name the compressed folder Lastname_Firstname_w7_SC_Zip as shown in **Figure 4**.

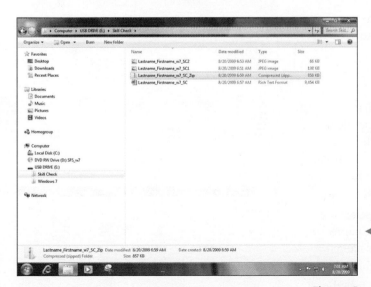

Figure 4

21. **Close** all open windows, and then **Close** the Slide Show gadget. Delete the **WordPad** shortcut and WordPad file from the desktop. Return the desktop to its original settings, and then remove the **Snipping Tool** icon from the taskbar. Submit as directed.

Done! You have completed the Skill Check

Assess Your Skills 1

To complete this project, you will need the following folder:

- 01_student_data_files

You will save your files as:

- Lastname_Firstname_w7_Skills1
- Lastname_Firstname_w7_Skills1_Snip1
- Lastname_Firstname_w7_Skills1_Snip2
- Lastname_Firstname_w7_Skills1_Zip

1. Add the **Weather** gadget to the desktop, and then set the location to your own city. Set the gadget to the larger size, and then position it in the lower left corner of the desktop.

2. Pin the **Snipping Tool** to the taskbar.

3. **Start** WordPad. If necessary, snap the WordPad window to the right edge of the desktop. In WordPad, type your first and last name, and then press Enter.

4. Open the **Computer** window, and then position and resize the window between the upper left corner of the desktop and the **WordPad** window and above the **Weather** gadget.

5. In the **Computer** window, display your USB drive or storage device file list, and then create a new folder named Assess Your Skills 1

6. Display the **Desktop Background** gallery, and then under **United States**, apply the first thumbnail.

7. Open the **Screen Saver Settings** dialog box, and then change the screen saver to **Bubbles**. Move the dialog box to the middle of the screen. Compare your screen with **Figure 1**, and then create a full-screen snip. **Save** the snip in your **Assess Your Skills 1** folder with the name Lastname_Firstname_w7_Skills1_Snip1 **Close** the dialog box and the **Personalization** window.

8. **Maximize** the **Computer** window, and then display the contents of the **01_student_data_files** folder located in the student CD. Sort the files by type, and then copy the 10 *Microsoft Office* files to your **Assess Your Skills 1** folder.

9. In your **Assess Your Skills 1** folder, rename the file **Volunteers** as Job Fair Volunteers and then delete the **Lightning** file.

10. Sort by **Name** in ascending order. Compare your screen with **Figure 1**, and then create a full-screen snip. **Save** the snip in your **Assess Your Skills 1** folder with the name Lastname_Firstname_w7_Skills1_Snip2

11. **Restore Down** your storage drive folder window. Drag the two snip files into the **WordPad** window. **Save** the WordPad file in your **Assess Your Skills 1** folder with the name Lastname_Firstname_w7_Skills1 If you are printing your work, print the WordPad document. **Close** WordPad.

12. In your **Assess Your Skills 1** folder, select the three files with your name in the file name, and then create a compressed folder named Lastname_Firstname_ w7_Skills1_Zip

13. **Close** all open windows, and then **Close** the **Weather** gadget. Delete the **Snipping Tool** shortcut, and then return the desktop to its original settings. Submit as directed.

Done! You have completed Assess Your Skills 1

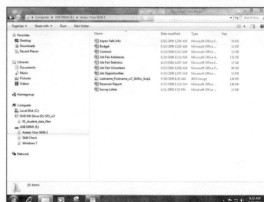

Figure 1

Assess Your Skills 2

To complete this project, you will need the following folder:

- 01_student_data_files

You will save your files as:

- Lastname_Firstname_w7_Skills2
- Lastname_Firstname_w7_Skills2_Snip1
- Lastname_Firstname_w7_Skills2_Snip2
- Lastname_Firstname_w7_Skills2_Snip3
- Lastname_Firstname_w7_Skills2_Zip

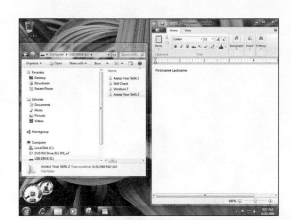

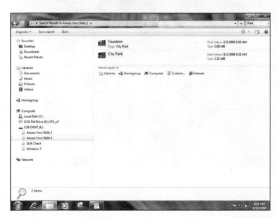

Figure 1

1. Add the **CPU Meter** gadget to the desktop and position it in the lower left corner of the desktop. Pin the **Snipping Tool** to the taskbar.

2. **Start** WordPad. If necessary, snap the **WordPad** window to the right edge of the desktop. In WordPad, type your first and last name, and then press Enter.

3. **Open** the **Computer** folder window, and then position and resize the window between the left edge of the screen and the **WordPad** window and above the **CPU Meter** gadget.

4. In the **Computer** window, display your USB drive or storage device file list, and then create a new folder named Assess Your Skills 2

5. Display the **Desktop Background** gallery, and then under **Nature**, apply the third thumbnail. **Close** the Personalization window.

6. Compare with **Figure 1**, and then create a full-screen snip. **Save** the snip in your **Assess Your Skills 2** folder with the name Lastname_Firstname_w7_Skills2_Snip1

7. **Maximize** the folder window, and then display the **01_student_data_files** file list located in the student CD. Copy the eight *JPEG image* files to your **Assess Your Skills 2** folder.

8. In your **Assess Your Skills 2** folder, rename the file **River1** as Aspen Falls River and then delete the **River2** file.

9. Sort by **Name** in ascending order, and then create a full-screen snip. **Save** the snip in your **Assess Your Skills 2** folder with the name Lastname_Firstname_w7_Skills2_Snip2

10. Tag the **Fountain** file with the text City Park

11. Search your **Assess Your Skills 2** folder for file names or file contents with the text Park

12. Compare your screen with **Figure 1** and then create a full-screen snip. **Save** the snip in your **Assess Your Skills 2** folder with the name Lastname_Firstname_w7_Skills2_Snip3

13. Display your **Assess Your Skills 2** file list and then **Restore Down** the folder window. Drag the three snip files into the **WordPad** window. **Save** the WordPad file in your **Assess Your Skills 2** folder with the name Lastname_Firstname_w7_Skills2 If you are printing your work, print the WordPad document. **Close** WordPad.

14. In your **Assess Your Skills 2** folder, select the four files with your name in the file name, and then create a compressed folder named Lastname_Firstname_w7_Skills2_Zip

15. **Close** all open windows, and then **Close** the **CPU Meter** gadget. Delete the **Snipping Tool** shortcut, and then return the desktop to its original settings. Submit as directed.

Done! You have completed Assess Your Skills 2

Assess Your Skills Visually

To complete this project, you will need the following file:

- New, blank WordPad document

You will save your files as:

- Lastname_Firstname_w7_AV
- Lastname_Firstname_w7_AV_Snip

Configure your desktop as shown in **Figure 1**. The desktop background is from the **United States** category, and the taskbar is on the right edge of the screen. In the upper left corner, add the **Control Panel** shortcut, and then arrange the three shortcuts as shown in the figure. In the upper right corner, add the **WordPad**, **Paint**, and **Calculator** shortcuts, and then arrange them as shown. In the lower left corner, add the **Currency**, **Calendar**, and **Clock** gadgets. Enlarge the **Currency** gadget and then arrange the three gadgets as shown in **Figure 1**.

On your USB flash drive, create a new folder named Assess Your Skills Visually and then close the Computer window. Compare your desktop with **Figure 1**, and then create a full-screen snip. **Save** the snip file as Lastname_Firstname_w7_AV_Snip Create a new **WordPad** document, add your name, and then drag the snip file into the **WordPad** window. **Save** the WordPad document in your **Assess Your Skills Visually** folder as Lastname_Firstname_w7_AV

Print the WordPad document or submit your files as directed by your instructor. Return the desktop to its original settings.

Done! You have completed Assess Your Skills Visually

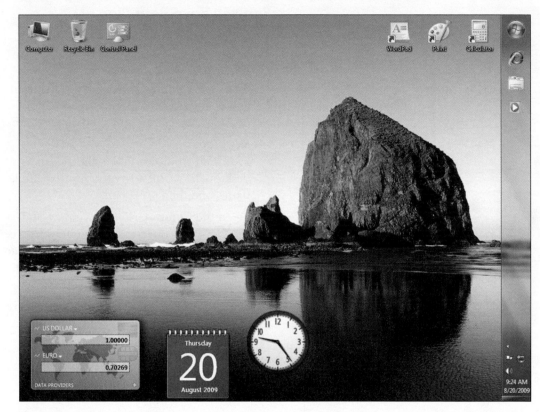

Figure 1

Skills in Context

To complete this project, you will need the following folder:

- 01_student_data_files

You will save your file as:

- Lastname_Firstname_w7_Context

The files in the folder *01_student_data_files* have work from three different projects. To organize these files, on your storage device, create a new folder named Skills in Context In the new folder, create three additional folders with the following names: Safety Presentation and Job Fair and Water Quality Search the *01_student_data_files* folder for file names and file contents for each project name. Then copy the files listed in the search results to the appropriate project folder. For example, search safety and then copy the four files from the student files to your **Safety Presentation** folder. Using this technique, you should find and move four files into the **Job Fair** folder and four files into the **Water Quality** folder.

Select your **Skills in Context** folder, and then create a zipped archive named Lastname_Firstname_w7_Context Submit the compressed folder as directed by your instructor.

If you are printing your work, create three snips showing the contents of each project folder. Then start WordPad, type your name, and drag the three snips into the WordPad window. Print the WordPad document, and close it without saving changes.

Done! You have completed Skills in Context

Skills and You

To complete this project, you will need the following files:

- Personal files stored on your computer

You will save your files as:

- Lastname_Firstname_w7_SY1
- Lastname_Firstname_w7_SY2
- Lastname_Firstname_w7_SY3

Use the skills you have practiced in this chapter to customize your computer's desktop. Change the desktop background and add at least one gadget that interests you.

If you have personal files that you have created outside of your work for this chapter, organize those files. Create new folders for each project and rename your files so that they clearly identify their contents. Move the files into the appropriate folders and delete files that are duplicates, old versions, or no longer needed.

Create a snip showing your desktop named Lastname_Firstname_w7_SY1 Then, create at least two more snips that illustrate your work to organize your personal files. Name each snip Lastname_Firstname_w7_SY2 then Lastname_Firstname_w7_SY3 and so on. Print the snips in a WordPad document, or submit the files electronically as directed by your instructor.

Done! You have completed Skills and You

Glossary

Accelerator A feature that searches for specialized information using the text you select on a Web page.

Accelerator A feature that searches the web for information related to the text you select.

Active content A program downloaded with a web page that provides additional functionality.

Active window The window in which typing or clicking occurs.

ActiveX script A small program that allows websites to provide content such as learning management systems.

Add-on A small program added to a browser to add functionality.

Adware Spyware that tracks your Internet browsing and can install malicious cookies on your computer.

Antispyware software A utility program used to search your hard drive for spyware and remove those that are found.

Antivirus software A utility program used to search your hard drive for viruses and remove those that are found.

Application software Programs that accomplish specific tasks, such as word processing, photo editing, or sending email and use the computer in a productive manner.

Arithmetic logic unit (ALU) Handles addition, subtraction, multiplication, and division, and also makes logical and comparison decisions.

Arrow keys Keys located at the bottom right of the keyboard between the standard keys and the numeric keypad that enable the user to move the insertion point around the active window.

Ascending order A sort order beginning with lower values and ending with higher values. For example, a to z.

Audio port Similar to video ports, these ports connect audio devices, such as speakers, headphones, and microphones to the computer's sound card.

AutoComplete A feature that stores the information and passwords that you enter into website forms so that you can automatically fill in other forms.

Backup A duplicate copy of computer files that can be used if the active copy is lost or damaged.

Backup tape drive A storage device used to save data to tape media resembling audiocassettes.

Bing Internet Explorer's default search provider.

Bluetooth A type of wireless technology that relies on radio wave transmission and doesn't require a clear line of sight. It is typically limited to less than 30 feet.

Boot process The process of starting up a computer; the computer begins when power is turned on.

Botnet Term associated with malicious software or software *robots*.

Browser See Web browser.

Browsing history The information that Internet Explorer stores as you browse the web.

Burn The process that saves data by using a laser beam that burns tiny pits into the storage medium.

CD burner Type of optical drive capable of reading and writing data from and to a CD (provided the media is recordable, like CD-Rs and CD-RWs).

CD-ROM CD media that was burned once and from that moment on can only be read.

CD-R Also known as CD-Recordable, a type of compact disk that can be recorded using a CD burner (drive).

CD-RW A rewritable disc that enables data to be recorded, revised, or deleted, and new data written to the disc, similar to magnetic media.

Central processing unit (CPU) The part of the computer responsible for controlling all the commands and tasks the computer performs, acting as the brain of the computer.

Click A mouse function in which you point at an object, press and release the left (or primary) mouse button once.

Click The action of pressing the left mouse button one time.

Client In a client/server network, the computer used at a desk or workstation to write letters, send email, produce invoices, or perform any of the many tasks that can be accomplished with a computer.

Client/server network A network in which two different types of computers have different functions. See also Client and Server.

Clipboard A temporary storage area from which you can paste an item.

Clock speed A measure of the speed at which a CPU processes data (number of instructions per second).

Communication and organizational software A program such as Microsoft Outlook 2007, used to send and retrieve email, manage day-to-day tasks such as appointments and contacts.

Compress To reduce the file size of one or more files into a single file that uses a .zip file extension.

Computer A programmable electronic device that can input, process, output, and store data.

Configure To put together by selecting a combination of components, features, and options.

Connectivity port Ports such as Ethernet and modem that are used to connect a computer to a local network or to the Internet.

Context-sensitive command An action commonly used when working with the selected object.

Control keys Keys such as the Cmd, Ctrl, Alt, and the Windows key that provide shortcuts or increased functionality to the keyboard when used in combination with other keys.

Control unit In the CPU, the component responsible for obtaining and executing instructions from the computer's memory.

Cookie A small text file written by a website. It is used to add functionality to the page or to analyze the way that you use the website.

Cookie A small text file that contains information that can identify you to a website.

CPU See Central processing unit.

Data Represents text, numbers, graphics, sounds, and videos entered to the computer's memory during input operations.

Database software Programs, such as Microsoft Access 2007, used to store and organize large amounts of data and perform complex tasks such as sorting and querying to generate specialized reports.

Data mining A function is some database software that looks for hidden patterns in the data to anticipate future trends.

Dedicated server A server in a network that is assigned to handle only specific tasks.

Default home page The page that first displays when you open a web browser.

Denial of service (DoS) Attacks that occur when a large number of computers try to access a website at the same time, effectively overloading it and causing it to shut down.

Descending order A sort order beginning with higher values and ending with lower values. For example, z to a.

Desktop The work area of the Windows 7 screen.

Desktop computer A class of microcomputer, such as a PC or a Mac, that typically occupies a working area around a desk.

Dialog box A box that asks you to make a decision about an individual object or topic.

Dialog box Windows used to make choices or give the system specific instructions as to the action you want to take or task to perform.

Digital camera A device that stores pictures digitally rather than using conventional film.

Digital Video Interface (DVI) port Ports that transmit a pure digital signal, eliminating the need for digital-to-analog conversion and resulting in a higher quality picture on an LCD monitor.

Digital video recorder Devices that let you capture digital images and movies and transfer them directly to your computer.

Docking station Device that enables the user to connect a notebook to a full-size keyboard, monitor, and other devices in an office setting.

Domain name A unique name assigned to a website on the World Wide Web.

DOS (Disk Operation System) The original OS for personal computers in the early 1980s. This was a text-based or keyboard-driven operating system.

Dot matrix Printers that have small hammers, similar to a typewriter's, that strike a ribbon against paper, leaving behind the image of a character or symbol.

Dot pitch A display characteristic in monitors that refers to the diagonal distance between two pixels of the same color. A smaller dot pitch results in a crisper viewing image because there is less blank space between the pixels.

Dots per inch (dpi) How resolution is expressed. The higher the dpi, the better the print quality.

Double-click The action of clicking and releasing the left mouse button twice in rapid succession while keeping the mouse still.

Drag To move the mouse while holding down the left mouse button and then releasing the button at the appropriate time.

Drag The action of moving something from one location on the screen to another; the action includes pointing and clicking (releasing the mouse button at the desired time or location).

DSL Acronym for digital subscriber line. Type of communications line in which signals travel through copper wires between a telephone switching station and a home or business.

Dual-core Processors that have several advantages over a single processor CPU, including improved multitasking capabilities, system performance, and lower power consumption.

DVD Acronym for Digital Video Disk or Diversified Video Disk; media that holds data written by an optical device.

DVD drive Digital Video Disk drive capable of reading and writing DVD media.

DVD-ROM DVD media that was burned once and from that moment on can only be read.

DVI port See Digital Video Interface.

Edit mode A mode in which you can change the name of a file or folder.

Embedded computers Small specialized computers built into larger components such as automobiles and appliances.

Ethernet port A port, slightly larger than a telephone jack, that can transmit data at speeds up to 1,000 megabits per second (Mbps) that is usually used to connect to a cable modem or a network.

Facebook A social networking website.

Favorite A stored web address that can be clicked to navigate to that page quickly.

Firewall A combination of hardware and software used to prevent unauthorized access to your computer.

FireWire port A port used to send data at rates up to 800 megabits per second (Mbps), frequently used for digital cameras or digital video recorders.

Flash drive A small, portable, digital storage device that connects to a computer's USB port (Universal Serial Bus); also called a thumb drive, jump drive, or USB drive.

Flash memory Portable, nonvolatile memory that uses electronic, solid-state circuitry.

Flat-panel displays Flat-panel displays or LCD monitors that use a liquid crystal display and are thin and energy efficient.

Floppy disk drive Device used to read and write to floppy diskettes media.

Floppy diskette Magnetic media used for data storage.

Form data Information that you have typed into forms, such as your logon name, e-mail address, and street address.

Function keys Keys that are located above the standard row of number keys and numbered F1 through F12. These keys are generally associated with certain software-specific commands.

Gadget A dynamic program that can be moved anywhere on your screen.

Gadget control A four-button tool set used to modify gadgets.

Gaming computers Computers that are mostly used by video game enthusiasts. They are usually configured with a fast CPU, large size memory, a special video card, sound card, and surround sound speaker system.

Gigabyte (GB) Approximately one billion bytes; a unit used to measure memory size and storage space.

Gigahertz (GHz) One billion hertz; a hertz is one of the units used to measure processor speed. One hertz is one cycle (instruction read) per second.

Graphical user interface An interface that uses graphics or pictures to represent commands and actions.

Graphical user interface (GUI) Today's operating systems provide a *user-friendly* way to operate a computer with their graphical user interface. The user controls the action using the keyboard, a mouse, or a touch screen to make selections from onscreen objects such as icons, menus, or dialog boxes.

GUI An acronym for graphical user interface.

GUI See Graphical user interface.

Hackers Derogatory term to describe individuals who gain unauthorized access to computer

systems for the purpose of corrupting or stealing data.

Handheld computers Small portable computers that might include personal productivity software and enable the user to play music, take photos and video, make phone calls, and access the Internet. PDAs, Pocket PCs, and smart phones fall in this category.

Hard copy The output of a printer (synonymous with printout).

Hard disk drive A combination of a device and media used as the main storage in most computers.

Hardware The physical or tangible components of the computer and any equipment connected to it.

Home page The starting point for the remainder of the pages at a website.

Hyperlink Any text or picture that can be clicked to move to a new page or location.

Hyperlink A connection to another area of a document or a connection to an Internet URL.

Hyperlink Text or a picture that moves you to a new location or Web page when it is clicked.

Icon A graphic representation of an object on the screen. Icons can be selected with the mouse or using your fingers on a touch screen.

IM Acronym for instant messaging, software that enables users to communicate in real time like a phone conversation but using text only.

Impact A type of printer that resembles a typewriter; a key punches an inked ribbon to imprint characters on paper.

Information Data that has been organized in a useful manner.

Information processing cycle The cycle composed of the four basic computer functions: input, process, output, and storage.

Inkjet A nonimpact printer that uses a special nozzle and ink cartridges to distribute liquid ink on the surface of the paper.

InPrivate A feature that prevents Internet Explorer from collecting information as you browse.

InPrivate Browsing An Internet Explorer window that limits the browser history that is written.

InPrivate filtering data Data used by InPrivate to determine if a website is sharing information about your visit.

Input During this step of the information processing cycle, the computer gathers data or allows a user to enter data onto memory.

Input devices Computer hardware used to enter data and instructions into a computer; examples include the keyboard, mouse, stylus, scanner, microphone, and digital camera.

Insertion point A blinking vertical line on the screen that shows where the next typed character will appear.

Internet control key Typically located at the top of certain keyboards, these keys enable the user to assign to each key a unique web browser functions such as sending email, browsing a specific site, or accessing an online bank account.

Internet Explorer The web browser provided by Windows 7.

Internet A global collection of networks that facilitate electronic communication such as e-mail, file sharing, and the World Wide Web.

Intranet A network or part of a network in which access is restricted to authorized users only.

IP address A unique set of numbers assigned to each computer on the Internet.

IrDA port A port that is used to allow devices such as PDAs, keyboards, mice, and printers to transmit data wirelessly to another device by using infrared light waves.

Joysticks Game controls that are input devices used to control movement within video games.

Jump list A list of related files or commands that you might jump to.

Key logger A type of spyware that records every keystroke made on the computer and can capture all sorts of confidential information this way such as passwords, credit card numbers, bank account numbers, and so on.

Keyboard The primary input device for computers.

Kilobit One thousand bits. It takes eight bits to make one byte.

LAN See Local area network.

Laser printer A type of nonimpact printer that uses a drum, static electricity, and a laser to distribute dry ink or toner on the surface of the paper.

LCD See Liquid crystal display.

Library A collection of files and folders stored at different locations on your computer that can be viewed as a single folder.

LightScribe A disc-labeling technology that burns text and graphics onto the surface of a specially coated LightScribe CD or DVD.

Linux An alternative operating system. It is open source software, which means it is not owned by a single company and some versions are available at no cost.

Liquid crystal display (LCD) Technology used in flat panel monitors, resulting in thinner, lighter monitors that consume less energy.

Local area network (LAN) A network in which the nodes are located within a small geographic area.

Local intranet Web content stored on internal networks that is accessed only by those within the organization.

Mac OS An operating system designed specifically for Apple's Macintosh computers.

Magnetic A type of storage process using magnetized film to store data; used by devices such as hard disks, or media such as tape cartridges.

Mainframe computers Computers often found in large businesses, organizations, and government agencies where thousands of users need to simultaneously use the data and resources for their everyday operations.

Malware A type of program designed to harm your computer, control your computer, or discover private information.

Maximize To enlarge a window to occupy the entire screen.

Megabit (Mb) Approximately one million bits. It takes eight bits to make a byte.

Megabyte (MB) Approximately one million bytes; a unit of measure for memory and storage space.

Megahertz (MHz) One million hertz; a hertz is one of the units used to measure processor speed. One hertz is one cycle (instruction read) per second.

Memory A generic term that signifies storage.

Menu A list of commands within a category.

Menu A list of commands that perform specific tasks within a program.

MHTML file Another name for a web archive.

Microcomputer The computer most users are familiar with and that ranges in size from large desktop systems to handheld devices. The name comes from its main component or brain called the "microchip" or microprocessor.

Microphones Input devices used to capture and record sounds.

Microprocessor chip A microcomputer's main component; it is a tiny but powerful chip compared to a mainframe or a supercomputer.

Microsoft Windows The operating system that runs most microcomputers today and provides a graphical user interface to make the computer "user friendly."

MIDI port Ports used to connect electronic musical devices, such as keyboards and synthesizers, to a computer.

Minimize To reduce a window to a button on the taskbar, removing it from the desktop without actually closing it.

Mobile devices These devices fall into the category of handheld computers; they are small enough to fit in the palm of your hand and enable users to access personal productivity software, send and read email, navigate the Internet; some are capable of wireless communications.

Modem port Ports used to connect a computer to a local network or to the Internet.

Monitor (or display screen) Display devices that show images of text, graphics, and video once data has been processed.

Monitor port A port that is used to connect the monitor to the graphics-processing unit, which is usually located on the motherboard or on a video card.

Motherboard A large printed circuit board located in the system unit to which all other boards are connected; the motherboard contains the central processing unit (CPU), the memory (RAM) chips, expansion card slots, and ports.

Mouse An input device (pointing device) used to enter commands and user responses into a computer. This device controls a symbol on the screen (mouse pointer) used to manipulate objects and select commands.

Mouse pointer In a graphical user interface environment, a pointer is a small arrow or other symbol on the screen that moves as you move the mouse. This lets the user make selections from objects on the screen such as icons, menus, or dialog boxes.

Multimedia control key Some modern keyboards have at least a few keys or buttons that can be used for such tasks as muting or adjusting speaker volume, opening a web browser, and sending e-mail.

Multimedia projectors Output devices used to display information on a screen for viewing by a large audience.

Multitask To perform more than one task simultaneously.

Navigation bar A vertical or horizontal bar with hyperlinks to the main pages of a website.

Network A group of two or more computers (or nodes) connected together via cables or wirelessly, to share information and resources.

Network topology The layout and structure of a computer network.

Node Any object connected to a network that is a computer or a peripheral device.

Nonimpact Printers that generate hard copies by means other than striking elements on to a ribbon and paper. They do not touch the paper when printing.

Nonvolatile Permanent storage; type of storage that holds its contents even when power is shut down. "Read Only Memory" (ROM) is a type of permanent storage.

Notebook computer Also known as a laptop, this microcomputer is smaller than a desktop and designed to be portable.

Numeric keypad A cluster of keys located at the right of the keyboard. This provides an alternative method of quickly entering numbers.

Open-source An operating system not owned by any company that can be changed by people with the appropriate programming knowledge.

Operating system Software that controls the hardware in your computer.

Operating system (OS) The software that controls the way the computer works from the time it is turned on until it is shut down.

Optical A type of storage process that uses a laser to read and write data, used to burn media such as CDs and DVDs.

OS See Operating system.

Output Data that has been processed and converted into information.

Output device Computer hardware components used to display information (show it) to the user; examples include the monitor, printer, and speakers.

P2P network (Peer-to-peer) A type of network in which each node can communicate with every other node. No PC has control over the network.

Parallel port A port that sends data in groups of bits as opposed to one bit at a time.

Peripheral A hardware device connected to a computer but not inside the system unit, such as a monitor, printer, a scanner, or mouse.

Permanent memory Type of memory that retains data and information even if the computer's power is turned off.

Personal firewall Software or hardware that, when installed properly, can make your computer invisible to hackers and other invaders.

Phishing website A dishonest website posing as a legitimate site to gain personal information, such as your logon and bank account number.

Pixel An abbreviated name for "picture element." Tiny dots that make up images on computer monitors.

Pixel The smallest dot of color in a picture, screen, or printout.

Pop-up A small window that displays in addition to the web page you are viewing.

Port An interface or a connecting point by which peripherals are connected to the computer's system unit.

Ppm Acronym for "pages per minute." A measure of the speed of a printer.

Presentation software A program, such as PowerPoint 2010, used to create dynamic slideshows and generate speaker notes and audience handouts.

Printer An output device used to generate hard copy or printout.

Printer friendly page An alternate web page that is designed to be printed.

Printout The output of a printer (synonymous with hard copy).

Privacy policy A document that explains what types of information is collected and how it will be used.

Process A CPU function in which data is converted into information.

Program Also known as software, sets of instructions or commands that tell the computer what to do and are used by the computer to perform certain tasks.

Programmable A device that can be programmed or instructed to perform a specific task guided by commands or instructions.

Protected Mode A feature that makes it more difficult for malware to be installed on your computer.

Public computer A computer that is available to others when you are not using it.

RAM A computer's temporary electronic memory.

RAM See Random Access Memory.

Random Access Memory (RAM) The computer's temporary storage space (short-term memory). It stores data on chips connected to the motherboard. This data is held just before processing by the CPU.

RDBMS Acronym for relational database management system and is database software that stores information in tables, which enable users quick access to the data by connecting tables with common fields.

Read Only Memory (ROM) See ROM.

Read/write Read is the action of retrieving or opening existing data and write is the action of saving or storing data.

Refresh rate The speed at which the screen's (monitor) image is redrawn.

Resolution The measurement used to assess the clarity and sharpness of an image on a monitor; determined by pixel density.

Restore To reduce a window to the size it was before being maximized.

Restore point A file in which all your computer system settings are stored. It's similar to taking a picture of how everything is currently set up. If there is a system failure, Windows can come to the rescue.

ROM Acronym for Read Only Memory. A type of memory prerecorded on a chip that the computer can only "read," not write or change its contents.

S-video port Short for Super-Video, a technology for transmitting video signals over a cable by dividing the video information into two separate signals, color and brightness.

Scanners Input devices used to convert hard copy documents or images into digital files.

Screen saver An animation that displays on your screen after a set period of computer inactivity.

ScreenTip A small note that describes a screen element.

Script Code downloaded with a web page that provides additional functionality.

Scroll bar A screen element added to the window whenever the window contains more content than it can display.

Scroll box A box in the scroll bar that provides a visual indication of your location within a window.

Search provider A website designed specifically for searching the World Wide Web.

Search provider A website that provides a way for you to search for information on the web.

Search results A list of suggested hyperlinks with descriptions of each page that they link to.

Search suggestion The words and phrases that display as you type in a search box.

Sectors Wedge-shaped sections of a hard disk drive or any magnetic storage media (ZIP disks and floppy disks), each measured from the center point to the outer edge.

Serial port Ports that can send data only one bit at a time.

Server In a client/server network, a server is the computer that manages shared network resources and provides access to the client computer when requested.

Shake To move a window back and forth quickly to open or close all other windows.

Site index A page of hyperlinks that outline a website.

Site map See Site index.

Shortcut An icon linked to another file or program that opens the file or program.

Shortcut menu A list of context-sensitive commands commonly used when working with the selected object.

Smartphones Handheld devices that combine mobile phone capabilities with other features typically associated with pocket PCs and PDAs.

SmartScreen Filter A feature that helps protect you from online threats.

Snip A screen shot captured using the Snipping Tool.

Snipping Tool A program that captures a screen or part of a screen.

Social networking website A site where people with similar interests share comments, photos, hyperlinks to web pages, and other information.

Soft copy The image generated by a display monitor as the result of output.

Spam Unwanted or unsolicited bulk email messages.

Speech recognition Technology that enables the user to record discussions or lectures, or to control the computer functions using voice commands.

Speakers Output devices that enable the user to hear any auditory signals the computer sends.

Splash screen A window used to inform the user of what kind of software is necessary in order to view a specific website. Also a window shown before a user is given the option to continue to the content of a website.

Spreadsheet software A program such as Microsoft Excel 2007 used to organize data in rows and columns, perform calculations, create charts, and perform numerical analyses.

Spyware Software designed to capture personal and confidential information that resides on your system and send it elsewhere.

Start menu A menu that gives you access to all the programs on your computer.

Storage Retention data or information for future use.

Storage devices Hardware components that retain data and information to be used in the future.

Stylus A pen-like input device used to write on a tablet computer or PDA.

Suite A collection of application software programs developed by the same manufacturer, bundled together and sold at a price that is usually less than the cost of purchasing each program individually. One example is Office 2010.

Supercomputer A large, powerful computer typically devoted to specialized tasks.

System software The set of programs that enables a computer's hardware devices and program to work together; it includes the operating system and utility.

System unit The tower, box, or console that contains the critical hardware and electrical components of a computer. Typically, the motherboard, the CPU, RAM, and the hard drive are contained within the system unit.

Tabbed browsing A feature that you use to open multiple web pages in the same browser window.

Tablet computer A portable computer that features a screen that swivels and can be written on using advanced handwriting recognition software.

Tag A custom file property that helps you find and organize your files.

Temporary Internet files Copies of web pages and their images stored in your personal folder. These are used to improve the time that it takes for frequently visited pages to display.

Temporary memory Short-term memory that stores data and program instructions that are waiting to be processed.

Terabyte One trillion bytes; a unit of measure for memory and storage space.

Toggle key Keystroke combinations that activate a function or, if pressed again, deactivate that function.

Top-level domain Letters after a domain name that specify the type of organization sponsoring a website—.gov, for example.

Touch screen A part of tablet computers that swivels and enables the tablet to be used like a standard notebook computer in one position or like a clipboard in the second position. These screens are considered input/output devices.

Touch screen technology A type of display screen that has a touch-sensitive panel, which enables the user to touch and make selections from onscreen objects using the tip of the finger.

TPL An acronym for Tracking Protection List.

Tracks Concentric circles on a hard disk drive or any magnetic storage media that together with sectors provide the storage space for data and information.

Tracking cookies Cookies that gather information about your web browsing behaviors.

Tracking Protection List An Internet Explorer add-on that helps prevent websites from collecting information about your visit.

Trojan horse A destructive program that presents itself as a genuine application.

Uniform Resource Locator The unique address of a page on the Internet.

Universal serial bus (USB) port A type of port able to interface with several different peripheral devices, which reduces the need for individual, dedicated ports.

URL An acronym for Uniform Resource Locator.

URL An address of a specific page on the Internet.

User friendly A user interface that can be used easily with minimum training because it provides visual aids and onscreen help for novice users.

User interface The feature of a computer's operating system that enables you to interact with the computer. Also see GUI (graphical user interface) and DOS (disk operating system text-based interface).

Utility program A component of system software, typically small programs used to perform routine maintenance and housekeeping tasks for the computer.

Video conferencing The use of networks to communicate audio and/or video between two or more individuals in different locations, optimizing communications, information sharing, and decision making.

Virus Malicious programs that are usually installed on your computer without your knowledge. Viruses can cause files to be corrupted or erased, are capable of shutting down a computer, or erasing the entire hard drive.

VoIP Acronym for Voice over Internet Protocol. Allows voice, facsimile, and voice-messaging communications over networks and the Internet.

Volatile Nonpermanent memory; type of storage that is lost when the computer is turned off.

WAN See Wide area network.

Web A nickname for the World Wide Web.

Web archive A file that saves web page text and pictures in a single file. These files are typically assigned the .mht file extension.

Web browser A program used to display Web pages and navigate the World Wide Web.

Web browser A program used to navigate the World Wide Web.

Web browser Software used to locate and display web pages and navigate through them.

Website A collection of connected pages located at a single domain name.

Wide area network (WAN) A network composed of local area networks connected over long distances.

Wiki A website that allows its members to edit existing pages and contribute as authors.

Window A frame on the computer screen that holds a program, a dialog box, or an object.

Window A rectangular box that displays programs, files, and folders.

Windows Explorer A program used to create and manage folders, and to copy, move, sort, and delete files.

Window name The name of a window that displays in the title bar.

Wireless Technology that transmits and receives data without a physical cable connection.

Wireless network A network that connects using radio waves instead of wires or cables.

Word processing software A program such as Microsoft Word 2010 used to create, edit, print, and save documents such as term papers, letters, forms, posters, and resumes.

World Wide Web A collection of linked pages designed to be viewed from any computer connected to the Internet.

Worm Similar to viruses, malicious programs that spread from computer to computer; however, unlike viruses, worms are able to do this without any human interaction and are able to replicate themselves.

WWW An acronym for World Wide Web.

Zombie A computer that can be controlled remotely by a hacker and can be used to spread viruses, spyware, or spam.

Index

 The internet icon represents Index entries found within More Skills
on the Companion Website: www.pearsonhighered.com/skills

153

Credits

Page 2: ifong/Shutterstock.

Page 4: Kurhan/Shutterstock.

Pages 5, 20, 21, 35, 43, 48, 55: Gaskin, Shelley; Giol, Victor, *Go! with Concepts Getting Started*, First Edition, © 2011. Reprinted by permission of Pearson Education, Inc., Upper Saddle River, NJ.

Page 6: Elnur/Shutterstock; Alex Staroseltsev/Shutterstock; Oleksiy Mark/Shutterstock; Mattia Terrando/Shutterstock.

Page 7: Dmitry Melnikov/Shutterstock (top); igorlale/Shutterstock (bottom).

Page 8: koya979/Shutterstock (top left), scherbet/Shutterstock (top right); ra2 studio/Shutterstock (bottom).

Page 9: blinkblink/Shutterstock (top); Oleksiy Mark/Shutterstock (bottom).

Page 10: Photosani /Shutterstock (top); Pell Studio (bottom).

Page 11: creativ000/Shutterstock.

Page 12: moritorus/Shutterstock.

Page 13: igorlale/Shutterstock (top); Dmitry Melnikov/Shutterstock (bottom left), terekhov igor/Shutterstock (bottom right).

Page 14: Oleksiy Mark/Shutterstock.

Page 15: Dusan Zidar /Shutterstock.

Page 17: Oleksiy Mark/Shutterstock (top); Laberta, Cathy, *Computers Are Your Future, Complete*, Twelfth Edition, © 2012. Reprinted by permission of Pearson Education, Inc., Upper Saddle River, NJ (bottom).

Page 18: Norman Chan/Shutterstock.

Page 18, 64: Geoghan, Debra, *Visualizing Technology, Complete*, First Edition, © 2012. Reprinted by permission of Pearson Education, Inc., Upper Saddle River, NJ.

Page 18, 63, 66: Beekman, George; Beekman, Ben, *Digital Planet: Tomorrow's Technology and You, Complete*, Tenth Edition, © 2012. Reprinted by permission of Pearson Education, Inc., Upper Saddle River, NJ.

Page 19: artizarus/Shutterstock.

Page 20: Your lucky photo/Shutterstock.

Page 21: Viktor Gmyria/Shutterstock.

Page 22: tkemot/Shutterstock.

Page 23: Grandpa/Shutterstock (top left), Graeme Dawes/Shutterstock (top right); luchschen/Shutterstock (bottom).

Page 24: Serg64/Shutterstock (top); kavione/Shutterstock (bottom).

Page 25: Goygel-Sokol Dmitry/Shutterstock.

Page 26: Doug Stevens/Shutterstock.

Page 27: Zadorozhnyi Viktor/Shutterstock (top); ~vvetc~/Shutterstock (bottom).

Page 28: janprchal/Shutterstock.

Page 29: Oleksiy Mark/Shutterstock (top left), Tatiana Popova/Shutterstock (top right); Péter Gudella/Shutterstock (bottom).

Page 30: Pavel Kirichenko/Shutterstock (top left), Thomas Staiger/Shutterstock (top right); Claudio Bravo/Shutterstock (bottom).

Page 31: Norman Chan/Shutterstock (top left), Inga Nielsen/Shutterstock (top right); Rafa Irusta/Shutterstock (bottom).

Page 32: Ivaschenko Roman/Shutterstock; Rafal Olkis/Shutterstock.

Page 33: Tim Arbaev/Shutterstock (top); John C. Hooten/Shutterstock (bottom).

Page 34: Valentin Mosichev/Shutterstock (top); Christopher Elwell/Shutterstock (bottom).

Page 35: SStiling/Shutterstock.

Page 36: lexan/Shutterstock (top); Alexander Kalina/Shutterstock (bottom).

Page 37: Szymon Apanowicz/Shutterstock (top); TEA/Shutterstock (bottom).

Page 38: Tootles/Shutterstock.

Page 42: jerrysa/Shutterstock.

Page 52: Screen shots © Intuit Inc. All rights reserved.

Page 54: sahua d/Shutterstock.

Page 56: 300dpi/Shutterstock, prism68/Shutterstock, Robert Milek/Shutterstock (top); gibsons/Shutterstock, Pearson Education (bottom).

Page 57: Kovalchuk Oleksandr/Shutterstock.

Page 67: Fotonium/Shutterstock.

Page 70: Evans, Alan R.; Martin, Kendall; Poatsy, Mary Anne S., *Technology in Action, Complete*, Eighth Edition, © 2012. Reprinted by permission of Pearson Education, Inc., Upper Saddle River, NJ.

SINGLE PC LICENSE AGREEMENT AND LIMITED WARRANTY

READ THIS LICENSE CAREFULLY BEFORE OPENING THIS PACKAGE. BY OPENING THIS PACKAGE, YOU ARE AGREEING TO THE TERMS AND CONDITIONS OF THIS LICENSE. IF YOU DO NOT AGREE, DO NOT OPEN THE PACKAGE. PROMPTLY RETURN THE UNOPENED PACKAGE AND ALL ACCOMPANYING ITEMS TO THE PLACE YOU OBTAINED THEM. *THESE TERMS APPLY TO ALL LICENSED SOFTWARE ON THE DISK EXCEPT THAT THE TERMS FOR USE OF ANY SHAREWARE OR FREEWARE ON THE DISKETTES ARE AS SET FORTH IN THE ELECTRONIC LICENSE LOCATED ON THE DISK:*

1. GRANT OF LICENSE and OWNERSHIP: The enclosed computer programs ("Software") are licensed, not sold, to you by Prentice-Hall, Inc. ("We" or the "Company") and in consideration of your purchase or adoption of the accompanying Company textbooks and/or other materials, and your agreement to these terms. We reserve any rights not granted to you. You own only the disk(s) but we and/or our licensors own the Software itself. This license allows you to use and display your copy of the Software on a single computer (i.e., with a single CPU) at a single location for academic use only, so long as you comply with the terms of this Agreement. You may make one copy for back up, or transfer your copy to another CPU, provided that the Software is usable on only one computer.

2. RESTRICTIONS: You may not transfer or distribute the Software or documentation to anyone else. Except for backup, you may not copy the documentation or the Software. You may not network the Software or otherwise use it on more than one computer or computer terminal at the same time. You may not reverse engineer, disassemble, decompile, modify, adapt, translate, or create derivative works based on the Software or the Documentation. You may be held legally responsible for any copying or copyright infringement which is caused by your failure to abide by the terms of these restrictions.

3. TERMINATION: This license is effective until terminated. This license will terminate automatically without notice from the Company if you fail to comply with any provisions or limitations of this license. Upon termination, you shall destroy the Documentation and all copies of the Software. All provisions of this Agreement as to limitation and disclaimer of warranties, limitation of liability, remedies or damages, and our ownership rights shall survive termination.

4. DISCLAIMER OF WARRANTY: THE COMPANY AND ITS LICENSORS MAKE NO WARRANTIES ABOUT THE SOFTWARE, WHICH IS PROVIDED "AS-IS." IF THE DISK IS DEFECTIVE IN MATERIALS OR WORKMANSHIP, YOUR ONLY REMEDY IS TO RETURN IT TO THE COMPANY WITHIN 30 DAYS FOR REPLACEMENT UNLESS THE COMPANY DETERMINES IN GOOD FAITH THAT THE DISK HAS BEEN MISUSED OR IMPROPERLY INSTALLED, REPAIRED, ALTERED OR DAMAGED. THE COMPANY DISCLAIMS ALL WARRANTIES, EXPRESS OR IMPLIED, INCLUDING WITHOUT LIMITATION, THE IMPLIED WARRANTIES OF MERCHANTABILITY AND FITNESS FOR A PARTICULAR PURPOSE. THE COMPANY DOES NOT WARRANT, GUARANTEE OR MAKE ANY REPRESENTATION REGARDING THE ACCURACY, RELIABILITY, CURRENTNESS, USE, OR RESULTS OF USE, OF THE SOFTWARE.

5. LIMITATION OF REMEDIES AND DAMAGES: IN NO EVENT, SHALL THE COMPANY OR ITS EMPLOYEES, AGENTS, LICENSORS OR CONTRACTORS BE LIABLE FOR ANY INCIDENTAL, INDIRECT, SPECIAL OR CONSEQUENTIAL DAMAGES ARISING OUT OF OR IN CONNECTION WITH THIS LICENSE OR THE SOFTWARE, INCLUDING, WITHOUT LIMITATION, LOSS OF USE, LOSS OF DATA, LOSS OF INCOME OR PROFIT, OR OTHER LOSSES SUSTAINED AS A RESULT OF INJURY TO ANY PERSON, OR LOSS OF OR DAMAGE TO PROPERTY, OR CLAIMS OF THIRD PARTIES, EVEN IF THE COMPANY OR AN AUTHORIZED REPRESENTATIVE OF THE COMPANY HAS BEEN ADVISED OF THE POSSIBILITY OF SUCH DAMAGES. SOME JURISDICTIONS DO NOT ALLOW THE LIMITATION OF DAMAGES IN CERTAIN CIRCUMSTANCES, SO THE ABOVE LIMITATIONS MAY NOT ALWAYS APPLY.

6. GENERAL: THIS AGREEMENT SHALL BE CONSTRUED IN ACCORDANCE WITH THE LAWS OF THE UNITED STATES OF AMERICA AND THE STATE OF NEW YORK, APPLICABLE TO CONTRACTS MADE IN NEW YORK, AND SHALL BENEFIT THE COMPANY, ITS AFFILIATES AND ASSIGNEES. This Agreement is the complete and exclusive statement of the agreement between you and the Company and supersedes all proposals, prior agreements, oral or written, and any other communications between you and the company or any of its representatives relating to the subject matter. If you are a U.S. Government user, this Software is licensed with "restricted rights" as set forth in subparagraphs (a)-(d) of the Commercial Computer-Restricted Rights clause at FAR 52.227-19 or in subparagraphs (c)(1)(ii) of the Rights in Technical Data and Computer Software clause at DFARS 252.227-7013, and similar clauses, as applicable.

Should you have any questions concerning this agreement or if you wish to contact the Company for any reason, please contact in writing:

Multimedia Production
Higher Education Division
Prentice-Hall, Inc.
1 Lake Street
Upper Saddle River NJ 07458